MAKE PROFESSIONAL DEVELOPMENT MATTER!

A GUIDELINE TO IMPROVE EDUCATORS

NICK SUTTON

Illustrated by
ADDI SUTTON

EduMatch
PUBLISHING

ISBN: 978-1-953852-32-8

This book is definitely dedicated to my family. Emily, Addi, Jack, Audrey and Olivia. I am not sure this book would exist if it wasn't for all of you!

CONTENTS

PREFACE

I suppose there are lots of reasons that individuals want to obtain a doctoral degree. First and foremost, something is satisfying about those two letters in front of your name. Anyone who says that is not something that is gratifying in itself to a certain extent, I would never totally believe. However, some individuals also work towards their doctorate for career advancement. Doing so definitely presents professional opportunities that would not have existed.

For me personally, I wanted to get my doctorate for a variety of reasons. Having the recognition for the accomplishment and the enhanced resume were definitely variables, but I also had a foundational reason I wanted to do the research. I was approximately halfway through an educational career in which I had been fortunate to have a lot of awesome experiences. I had taught at a few different and rewarding settings and then was humbled to have also climbed the administrative ladder to become a principal and then district superintendent.

During this journey, I had developed and evolved philosophies like any other educator. One area that I had become focused upon, especially when I became an administrator, was the necessity to have a positive culture in district settings. In many ways, I had reached a point of conclusion that culture was the most important area of focus for any educational site. After a while, this perspective had even developed into a skill set, as well. I was good at and certainly saw the importance of perpetuating and nurturing an environment of positivity.

My other aspect of educational leadership focus is perhaps the basic reason we even exist as educators. This would be student achievement. I worked hard to have this area become a passion of mine, and it definitely has gotten to that point for me. While serving teachers in a leadership position, there will be those with varying levels of expertise, interest, and viewpoints. However, the one constant and universal common area of interest for all teachers will be instruction intended to impact student learning. All teachers, no matter the content or grade level, utilize instruction, so it was this overarching connection that I found really attractive.

This summary of experiences was the catalyst for when it became time to select the topic of my dissertation research. I knew that a positive culture was obviously important, and I also knew that some instructional strategies were better than others. I began wondering to the point of obsession if there were some instructional strategies that my research would indicate that could not only increase student achievement, but their consistent utilization with students would also correlate to creating a setting with a positive culture.

The thought of discovering this connection seemed like the answer I had always been looking for. Imagine being able to stand in front of a group of teachers and show them research that indicated if you embrace these types of teaching strategies, you would also perpetuate an environment of happiness and achievement. How then could anyone argue there not being a need to use these strategies? Wouldn't this then be information that could benefit literally every school in existence?

While this beginning goal of my research seemed a bit lofty, now as I reflect, it perpetuated a journey of realization that at a minimum has positively impacted me. As I was collecting the data to examine the core question of my doctoral work, the eventual conclusion was not what I initially expected. Essentially, I could not connect that using certain instructional strategies would then directly align to perpetuating a positive climate. While initially dismayed, I then realized that this information demonstrated and led me towards other realizations that were just as important.

Based on this experience, the idea for this book was born. This book is a collection of not only my doctoral work, but also my blog posts, tweets, graduate coursework papers, and professional thoughts I have had during the evolution of my career. These results have allowed me to create a research-based guide to impact student achievement through a blueprint for building professional development plans. This conclusion then allowed me to discover perhaps the most direct manner to improve a school's culture. Originally, I researched within my dissertation to see if there was a correlation between some instructional strategies and a positive school culture. In the process of doing this work though, I ended up discovering an entirely different conclusion than I thought I would and these findings then evolved into this book. In other words, while I initially set out to find the answer to one challenge, I ended up finding an answer to an entirely different question I had never even asked.

SECTION 1: WHY DOES SOME OF OUR SOCIETY ENJOY SEEING PEOPLE FAIL?

Why do some people in our society seem to enjoy seeing others fail? Perhaps, even posing this question may seem bizarre and disconnected from a book that is advertised about discussing professional development. I would certainly acknowledge that this would seem like a strange relationship to establish, but for me, this seems like a foundational point to make.

I genuinely believe that there are individuals in our society that take solace when others struggle. Perhaps this is a bit of a negative position. Rest assured though, this is not my goal at all. Instead, I think the first step to solving a problem is simply acknowledging the existence of the problem itself.

If an educator will improve, it is because of quality professional development. However, they also have to have the mindset that they want to do so. Schools are no different than the challenges society faces as a whole. As such, we have to accept that not everyone is at a point all the time where they want to see others, or maybe even themselves, succeed. Educators are awesome individuals that selected the greatest career in the world, but they are also subject to the challenges we all face personally, and these can certainly take a toll.

HUMAN NATURE AND EDUCATORS

*E*ducators become educators because they want to make an impact. They want to help others. They want to make a positive difference in students' lives. I also truly believe that almost all individuals, in whatever other career field, begin life wanting to improve the world that we live in. What becomes the question to consider is why this changes for some people and for others it does not. In other words, what happens that makes some educators lose the instinctive purpose in life to make impactful contributions to their students?

The purpose of this book is not to create the debate on whether or not human beings are inherently good or bad, or whether or not my above premise is accurate. Instead, I want to focus upon the undeniable notion that some people help others and some people do not. At this point, anyone reading this part of this book can automatically begin imagining people that they would place into either of these categories.

There are endless variations that one could argue within these two areas of human nature, and there are also limitless variables on how and why people end up within, or near, one of the ends of these spectrums, as well. However, the purpose of this chapter is to examine how some professional educators enter a field having a positive outlook and perspective only to eventually end up having anything but.

We live in a world where people enjoy, or at a minimum, are interested when bad things happen to other people. Whenever we know someone that gets arrested, has a breakdown, or goes through a traumatic event, why does this garner such curious attention from society as a whole? Some would argue that it perhaps is a sick fascination in general. However, I think the true reason and premise is something much deeper, and something that also affects all educators, as well.

I believe educators live in a world in which their profession is driven by the perception that if someone is going to educate another, then the educator should be an individual that is inherently an expert in content and also perfect a human being. The rhetorical question in many minds becomes, "How can a teacher that is anything but perfect on a personal level possibly be appropriate to teach others?"

Perhaps some teachers are driven by the misconception that they must always be distinguished, and never show any type of weakness, because there is a collective realization that our society takes a bizarre interest in seeing others also fail. Maybe educators who have realized that they are actually anything but perfect then take collective comfort that others are far from perfect, as well. However, the fear of then acknowledging their own shortcomings makes them unreceptive to any opportunities to become better educators.

2

SOCIETY TAKES COMFORT IN OTHERS'
FAILURES

*W*e all grew up in various time periods that are marked by events that become memorable to us for whatever reasons. Despite our ages or backgrounds, this human and instinctive connection is universal. For example, if someone grew up during the Kennedy assassination, they will clearly remember this and the societal perceptions of this time. In turn, if someone was not alive during this event, but was for September 11, they will remember this event in the same way, as well.

Now I have a large volume of interesting memories relative to society, too. Some of the ones that come to my mind for this example are driven by pop culture more than anything else. I largely grew up in the 1990s and 2000s, and as such, have a lot of memories relative to this time period with various actors, musicians, etc.

Like any other individual, I can think of various celebrities from this point in time that ended up having issues that were anything but positive. What is interesting to me is why it is so engaging for our society when something unfortunate happens to a celebrity past their prime. I think it is intriguing especially when it is a former celebrity that has also been receiving no recognition for anything else for some time. Consider thinking of a famous actor or actress that slowly dissipated from public view because their 15 minutes of fame had run its course. However, if something significantly detrimental happens to them, even if it has been decades since anyone in society has acknowledged their former status, it is always an immediate story.

A good example that comes to my mind would be the singer Britney Spears. I grew up in the 1990s, and during this time period, she was certainly a very well-known singer that many, including myself, certainly knew about. However, as her career started to wind down as every celebrities' career inevitably does, she became more famous than she ever was when her life began facing significant challenges. I can still recall the point years ago when it seemed like every day there was another photo of her in an unfortunate situation or a story about something bad happening to her. Perhaps the pinnacle of this difficult part of her life was when photographers captured the time she decided to shave her head.

While I could only imagine what was going through her mind, it is impossible to not surmise that she was at a personal breaking point. Sadly, it seemed as though society as a whole was not collectively coming together to help or support her. Instead, we as a society were collectively salivating for the next unfortunate instance she would produce for our amusement and interest.

It is not that I do not understand the allure. Whenever one of us personally reflects on our own lives, when compared to an incredible and successful celebrity, it is easy to feel inferior, or to have self-assessments of failure, even if they are not accurate or fair. In many ways, it may be part of being a human being whether we want to admit it or not. We compare ourselves to others, and when we encounter others that we feel are superior to us, we take at least a little comfort when it comes out that they are anything but.

When contemplating this topic, I like to even take it a step further for reflection. I would challenge anyone to think of a musician, actor, politician, etc. who was once on the top of the world that eventually found themselves fall totally flat for whatever reason. It doesn't matter who it is, as long as it is a celebrity who finds themselves within the unfortunate cycle in which they are famous and doing great and then they find themselves embroiled in turmoil. Now reflect and ask yourself how and why then during the downturn the person became more famous than they ever were before. Is it because the issue itself is more interesting to society than anything else they ever did? Or is it because it makes others feel better about themselves, as well?

3

IS THERE ALSO THIS TYPE OF ATMOSPHERE AT SCHOOLS?

*a*s an educator with about 15 years of experience, I have crossed paths with so many different individuals it is impossible to keep track. I now know countless teachers, principals, and superintendents, and I love knowing that I do. There is something wonderful and powerful that if I ever want advice or have a question related to the education field, I have no lack of individuals I can reach out to.

Obviously, every school district and community is different with their core values, and frankly, they should be. I am a tremendous advocate of local control and for school boards to be able to govern in the manners their community norms wish. However, there are also a wide variety of common aspects that all schools should institute, and these types of aspects are met with unspoken and universal expectations of embracement.

For example, there is not (at least I hope) a school in existence that doesn't value teaching a phonics-heavy reading curriculum at the early grade levels. This is a common and shared core value. In other words, it would be unheard of if this wasn't happening. While this perspective can be surmised with a variety of positive aspects for a school, there are also universal negative core values that are instilled at virtually all schools, as well.

A specific strange norm that exists in schools is the seemingly same norm that exists within society for celebrities. In other words, when something unfortunate happens, it is met with more interest than anything else. At one point in my career, I was affiliated with a district that had multiple schools. Each school in the district had its own challenges and items to be proud of, but also its own identity and perceptions. One school, in particular, had a large volume of positive initiatives happening that had wonderful effects on kids. The building should have been, by all accounts, a school that was only known for positive reasons.

Interestingly though, this could not have been further from the truth. This school had an administrator who was known for poor decisions both professionally and personally, and no matter what wonderful action that the school was implementing, no one ever seemed to take notice. Sadly, when this administrator's time leading this building finally met its demise with him being fired, I watched this situation become the most interesting and talked about topic that this school ever had.

I realize someone being terminated from their job will always be met with collective interest at least for no other reason than morbid curiosity. However, what I eventually began finding disturbing is why it took something so ugly and so unfortunate to finally get the attention of the community while the rest of the school was working so tirelessly to convey positive outcomes. I sometimes still reflect on this occurrence because I feel like this school is still more known today for this unfortunate event, even though it has now been years since this originally happened.

I think what bothered me more than anything was how district staff partook in this negative gossip with a level of interest and engagement. It was amazing because this type of commitment wasn't being utilized to communicate all of the positive items happening, but when the opportunity for the latter came to be, this had immediate follow-through.

To a certain degree, I can understand why something negative happening is interesting, but what I cannot fathom is why others seem to take pleasure when something like this occurs. More importantly, I find it fascinating why this phenomenon takes place in schools. Schools are the settings in which society empowers educators to prepare their youth to develop into productive adults. In addition, these are the settings that are tasked with addressing the social-emotional needs of its student body while having the goal of eradicating bullying. Unfortunately, we as a society also have these negative types of norms in our schools. No one is asking how this came to be, why is this allowed, and most importantly, how this could indirectly or directly affect kids.

Educators are incredible people, and I feel honored to say this is a career field that I am a part of. We have stressful, overwhelming, and sometimes anxiety-filled positions, but I sometimes feel remiss that maybe we also forget that we have exciting, impactful and life-changing opportunities with our positions. However, I simply do not know of an educator that hasn't experienced some of the negative experiences I outline above. By acknowledging that this does happen, it isn't meant to be a slight on educators. Instead, it is meant to be a step towards addressing an unfortunate norm that all of us in this field are aware of and embracing how it could have a negative effect.

4

DO WE FEEL BETTER WHEN WE THINK WE ARE SOMEHOW BETTER THAN OTHERS?

*Y*ears ago, I took my two daughters to a large cheerleading competition. If any other parents reading this book have been to an event like this, they know how large some of these events truly are. This particular one took place near Chicago and was intense due to the volume of spectators, to say the least.

While there were a lot of wonderful memories during this weekend event, one experience that has been burned into my mind was certainly not positive, but as I continue to reflect on this day now years later, it was not necessarily a negative event either. Instead, it was thought-provoking, and truly enough so that I still find myself reflecting on it even today.

When traveling home, we were in a large enough area near the Chicago suburbs that there were people everywhere, and the volume of cars only seemed to increase as we neared the highway. As we approached the last set of stoplights, right before the entrance to the onramp to the side of the road there was an individual holding a sign that indicated that he was homeless and was asking for money. As I instinctively noticed the individual right away, I wasn't sure how my two young children were going to react. At the time, my oldest was about 7 years old, putting her right at the correct age to have questions, but also not entirely able to understand the predicament the poor person along the road had found himself in.

"What does homeless mean?" my daughter asked.

I can still remember that my child asked me this question in a manner and tone that I will never forget, but also with a level of confused innocence that made this instance for me a memory that will remain. I went on to explain that sometimes individuals simply aren't born with the privileges that some of us are and that sometimes individuals have horrible and unfortunate things happen to them that contribute to a difficult situation. Basically, I stumbled through the standard answer that most would imagine an un-expecting parent to give when tasked to answer a question of this potential scope and magnitude.

While many of the specific details of this experience are now lost upon me, the one takeaway I do recall though was the concluding comment I made at the end was something I was initially quite satisfied with.

"This is really unfortunate that this person is in this situation. It's too bad, and this should really make us feel appreciative of all that we have," I explained.

Now at first, I am presuming that individuals out there that are reading this may be wondering what is wrong with this response. Perhaps, many reading right now are even becoming curious where I am going with this because this comment could maybe be very similar to a comment they would make themselves if in a similar situation with their own children.

I felt pretty content with how I handled this, too.... initially.

However, as I continued to drive back home, it occurred to me that I felt content by stating to my children that I was officially "not okay with the homeless person's situation and felt bad that he was in the predicament that he was in." I did not do anything to actually help him though. I didn't offer him any direct assistance, I didn't offer him any money, and I certainly did not actually do something that was going to help his plight. Instead, I just made it known that I felt bad.

This experience, while seemingly remote, deeply made a strange impression on me because I think this is an approach that is taken in both public education and society as a whole. For example, I want every educator at this point to imagine a student they knew in school that had a horrible home life and difficult time in school, but perhaps also wasn't in their own actual class. Now I am sure there are exceptions, but how many of us can now realize that their approach to feeling content with the situation was to feel sorry for the child, but never actually follow through to do something to truly help them.

To take this a step further, I want to provide a dramatic example to further exemplify my point. I want to bring up the topic of racism. Outside of a very few stupid people, there is almost no one that does not find this practice horrendous (and also idiotic). However, I find that myself, and most people, are in a position with this type of topic that they are content to simply let it be known that "they are against it." My fear then becomes how few individuals are actively and aggressively looking to improve or address it. Instead, so many individuals are content to simply acknowledge that a social injustice, such as this, is something we do not support. This makes us feel content. This makes us feel okay. This makes us feel as though we have done enough.

Social dilemmas seem to all fit within three levels of position. The lowest position is indicative of ignoring the issue's existence. I think of this as the "Indifference Level." The mid-level is making it known you are against a social injustice, and certainly not pretending that it doesn't exist, but at best, advocating for more awareness. I think of this as the "Typical Level." Lastly, the highest level involves action to actually address the issue itself. It involves equipping and arming ourselves with substance and determination to create change. This is the "Action Level."

I hate seeing this, but I fall within the "Typical Level" of my before-mentioned definitions if I honestly self-assess myself in many instances. There are so many of us that fall into this realm because it is easier to focus on a problem than to address it. In addition, since most in our society would fall into this mid-level range, there is also solace of being within the group that has the most participants. However, I see now that nothing positive will occur while being in this position, and as an educational leader, I need to expect more from myself.

There is an extraordinary relationship between this analogy and public education. Is this why some educators are not driven to improve or address issues? Is this type of perspective why some people think just "being against" something is enough without actually doing something to address it?

5

THE RELATIONSHIP TO
PROFESSIONAL DEVELOPMENT

*T*he connection that the levels of social justice action has with professional development has been powerful for me to realize. There is an aspect of human nature that is comfortable with only acknowledging that something isn't okay, and not actually doing something to directly improve the issue. I truly think this is a variable on why some educators are not receptive to improving themselves through professional development. Since the 1970s there has been an explosion of research in the field of education. With any issue or challenge a school could be facing, there is an answer in existence that can be applied. However, simply providing a potential solution to a problem is not enough.

When I first became an administrator, I used to find the thought of leading staff meetings for the purpose of improvement through professional development really stressful. However, like anything else, I have become more and more comfortable doing these kinds of leadership activities. Interestingly though, there seem to be universal commonalities with these types of meetings that I have also learned firsthand through this journey. Among all of the various school districts that I have worked within or discussions I have had with other educators in my professional network about their own districts, one particular aspect that I am referring to is the type of educator attending professional development who decides that no matter what the topic, explanation or demonstration of the need to change, they are against it.

We have all met these kinds of educators (and hopefully no one is realizing that I am describing them). They are the person that ignores data. They are the person that ignores research. They are the person that is able to have as many excuses as necessary on why they do not need to change.

For the longest time, I was a person that always equated and justified the existence of these people by taking the stance that they were just unenlightened or negative. It wasn't until my previously described experience with my daughters and the homeless gentleman that I realized the three levels of social justice action could have a relationship to the audiences of professional development, too.

For example, I want everyone to imagine that they are sitting in a school staff meeting. Everyone is there and an administrator is in the middle of a presentation describing some concerning issue. The administrator is prepared and dynamic, and most importantly, is showing some undeniable data that is impossible to argue. Let's suppose they are showing that this school has an achievement gap between low-income and non-low-income students and is providing an in-depth justification on why practices need to change.

Now with this imaginative predicament, I want everyone to also imagine one unconvinced staff member sitting with their arms crossed in the corner of the room despite the data that essentially proves the need. Their body language indicates their distaste and disapproval of the potential change being suggested. However, is this individual basing their displeasure not so much on the idea itself, or even the specific new practice being suggested, but instead because they are content simply thinking that an achievement gap is not okay? Or are they just not at a place in which they feel the need to actually do anything? In other words, are they content merely thinking the issue is not alright, but are not driven enough to actually want to work towards solving it? Are they at the "Typical Level" of action for a social injustice within the guidelines I described previously?

SOCIAL JUSTICE LEVELS OF ACTION

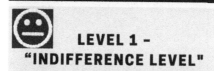

LEVEL 1 – "INDIFFERENCE LEVEL"

AN INDIVIDUAL THAT HAS NO RESERVATIONS ABOUT A BLATANT SOCIAL INJUSTICE. THEY EITHER DO NOT SEE AN ISSUE OR EVEN MORE CONCERNING, DO NOT CARE.

LEVEL 2 – "TYPICAL LEVEL"

AN INDIVIDUAL THAT ACKNOWLEDGES SOCIAL INJUSTICE EXISTS AND THAT IT IS ALSO INAPPROPRIATE. HOWEVER, THEY DO NOT ACTIVELY DO ANYTHING TO IMPROVE OR SOLVE THE ISSUE. THEY FEEL CONTENT BY LETTING IT BE KNOWN THAT THEY ARE AGAINST AN INJUSTICE.

LEVEL 3 – "ACTION LEVEL"

AN INDIVIDUAL THAT IS NOT CONTENT BY MERELY THINKING AN ISSUE IS INAPPROPRIATE. INSTEAD, THE ISSUE ITSELF MOTIVATES THIS PERSON TO WANT TO SEE THE ISSUE SOLVED. THEY ARE NOT CONTENT AS LONG AS THE ISSUE EXISTS.

BY: DR NICK SUTTON

6

HOW DOES OUR SOCIETY AFFECT
EDUCATIONAL IMPROVEMENT?

P. J. Palmer discusses the decline of public life within his work, *Healing the Heart of Democracy: The Courage to Create a Politics Worthy of the Human Spirit* (2011). Although I feel it is safe to assume that the purpose of this book was never driven by any intention for an indirect connection to educational professional development, I found that the analogies he provides in this work helped me. After reading this, I found myself building connections about society, human nature, and the education field as a whole. For example, he observes how our society has seen malls replacing city streets and the demise of settings where strangers can interact freely. It used to be that settings such as these are where people shared information, ideas and even problem-solved at times (Palmer, 2011). Based upon this premise, if opportunities for face-to-face interactions are declining, and people are tending to choose activities that do not make freely shared ideas to be as possible for discussion as they once were, then why should educational leaders be surprised when creating a culture of collegial and collective improvement is so difficult?

Palmer also discusses how seclusion essentially leads towards a lack of information, and then, in turn, a lack of problem-solving. Upon initially reading about this perspective, it definitely made me introspective about myself as an educational leader. Specifically, does this also mean that the perspectives that I naturally have within my own experiences, both professionally and personally, is why I see the world through the view that I do? Or to take this a step further, are the issues, challenges, and even social dilemmas that a school encounters all defined relatively by who the leader of a school is?

Palmer believes that many of us are living in isolation and then are blind to possible approaches to address an issue. I think this statement is accurate and applies dramatically to public education. For example, I see now that parts of myself as an educational administrator living in a type of isolation, and under this environment, I am blind to see and understand certain realities and lifestyles. I pride myself on being successful working within diverse educational settings, but that experience certainly has not equipped or allowed me to solve all of the challenges I naturally face.

"In a healthy democracy, public conflict is not only inevitable but prized. Taking advantage of our right to disagree fuels our creativity and allows us to adjudicate critical questions of many sorts: true versus false, right versus wrong, just versus unjust" (Palmer, 2011, p. 61). I feel that most, if not all, educational leaders would agree with this statement. However, as I continue to work in this field and observe educators that do not improve for whatever reason, I am beginning to wonder if perhaps a variable is because no one can completely reach their potential unless they are in an atmosphere that supports some volume of discomfort based upon the very drive to change.

7

BEING AN ETHICAL ANALYST

R.J. Nash discussed that he wanted his students to become "ethical analysts." By them doing so, they then become individuals that have a perspective in which they can do more than merely identify cultural and societal issues (Nash, 1996). The goal would be for them to actually become individuals who potentially understand the issues our society faces. As an educational leader, I cannot think of a more powerful culture for a staff than one that is comfortable examining all of the social dilemmas that we will naturally encounter because then we can project that type of atmosphere onto the student body. Then, in turn, if this was the true reality of a school, how could anyone not be receptive to improving practice to benefit students?

I am not a true ethical analyst by any definition, but as I continue to grow, I certainly would love to one day become one. However, part of my personal saving grace for this topic is that this realization has come over time and that it needed to become an important variable to address within myself. This approach to leadership then equates to a true servant leadership style. Specifically, I believe it aligns with approaching issues in an effort to respond than merely react.

One quote from Nash's work that I think is critical to the point I want to make would be, "Why do you abstract out of our lives all the truly important stuff when you teach us how to resolve ethical dilemmas? It is like you are teaching us to write by giving us only nouns, but no adverbs, adjectives, or verbs!" (Nash, 1996, p. 58).

Personally, I like this comment because I feel like it implies that ethical dilemmas and social injustices are many times just examined and never truly delved into. I think there is much truth to this notion. There is an unspoken and rhetorical expectation perhaps within our society that only acknowledging an issue exists is enough. It is only when someone actually attempts or proposes a possible solution that has the potential to become messy that it then gets the attention of many. It is this messiness that probably frightens some. This interpretation is what I use as a take-away from "giving us only nouns, but no adverbs, adjectives, or verbs!"

I am starting to realize that Nash's perspective applies to the field of education by exposing educators to quality professional development. Educators that do not see or realize the power and purpose behind improvement through professional development is an issue. Seeing the problem itself is not difficult, but doing something about it is what is necessary. Just acknowledging that it exists is not enough.

8

EDUCATORS NEED TO BE CATALYSTS FOR CHANGE

*D*arling-Hammond and Rothman examined what it actually means to prepare future teachers well. Their conclusions spotlight how eventual educators need to be instructors that ensure their classrooms are inquiry-based for the benefit of their students (Darling-Hammond & Rothman, 2015). Establishing that classrooms need to be inquiry-based is not a new concept to many educators. This is a position that is well-grounded within many well-known topics of educational research.

However, I think having an emphasis on teacher's pedagogical approaches is what needs to be focused upon if we have hope for teachers of tomorrow to be future initiators of change. We need to use this approach to empower ourselves within this field. There is no other way to instill within the student populations that we work with to see that they have the capacity to improve issues in our culture.

R.J. Nash has stated, "What bothers character educators about applied ethical analysis and moral reasoning is that teachers such as I assume that students can learn to make good moral decisions without bothering to acquire moral habits or strength of character" (Nash, 1996, p. 162). I love this view. We, as educators, have to show our students how to analyze society if it is our goal to instill in them the drive, under-standing, and tools to improve it.

I have adapted and changed as a person like every other individual. Experiences that have been both positive and negative have shaped me as a person and made me into who I am today. Like everyone else, I have my own personal values and approaches to life that have been constructed over time. What I am beginning to realize is that I haven't been taking near enough ownership as an educational leader that has the power to institute change. I am able to modify programs, select staff, institute new instructional strategies, etc. However, the students and families that I work with and want to help may not realize the capacity I have to ensure change takes place for their benefit.

Addressing poor instruction in a school, and even then indirectly improving social dilemmas, is something I do control. The students and families may not have this ability to institute change, so expecting them to will only create stress and solve nothing. I need to see them as partners and counterparts for change, but not the ones that necessarily are supposed to initiate it.

Summary

I began this book by asking why others take some type of comfort in seeing others fail. This question becomes more than complex, and perhaps part of it is best to remain only rhetorical in nature. In other words, maybe this is a question that isn't meant to be answered.

However, I think exploring the relationship between this question and why some educators are not more driven to solve issues within their school is necessary. I am starting to believe more and more that people simply feel better by living in a state in which they can see themselves as within the mid-range of social injustice positions. The mid-range is not the worst, not the best, but a safe place to be.

The notion that individual educators possibly take comfort in being within this mid-range is interesting to me. By being in the second level of my Social Justice Levels of Action, does this perpetuate and sustain a culture within public education that we are not necessarily driven to be the best, but instead we are driven to just not be the worst? And by having this culture, improving through professional development may be impossible if we have staff that is genuinely satisfied being in this second level of action.

SECTION 2: THE FALLACY OF THE PERFECT EDUCATOR

I love educators, and after being an administrator in multiple different districts for over a decade, I have reached a point of having broad assumptions about educators in general. Assumptions are opinions and

shouldn't be misinterpreted as objective positions but they do have merit when based upon direct experience.

While there are always exceptions, I have continued to encounter resistance for some educators to truly see that no matter how good they are, that it isn't good enough to become complacent. There is always more we can do, something new we can be trained on, or a new practice we could perfect. This realization can be overwhelming, but we have to instead see it as a reason the field of education is so great. There is not a pinnacle of perfection that can be reached. Rather, we have to strive to always improve through professional development, and acknowledge that it is a never-ending journey.

9

HAVE I ALWAYS BEEN MY BEST?

*H*ave I always been my best? No. Absolutely not. Not even close. However, what I have realized is that more than anything I have spent an inordinate amount of time trying to pretend that I am always at my best. In other words, trying as best that I could to confuse the ratio between always being a professional (which is important and necessary) with also being an imperfect human being (which we all are, but sometimes forget).

I think the reason educators resist professional development may also contribute to why educators feel as though they have to pretend they are always at their best personally. And in some ways, this notion makes sense. If an educator is supposed to be someone that has enough skill or knowledge to instill information upon someone else, shouldn't they also be someone that is perfect in all aspects of life? Seeing this perspective in written words seems obviously ridiculous; however, I do think people sometimes place this unreasonable expectation upon themselves. I know that I have made the mistake of doing so.

I certainly have had periods of my professional life in which I have also not been at my best personally. Sadly, though, when experiencing these points in our life, the last thing we many times want to do is actually acknowledge that we are going through a challenging experience. By doing so, it leads to facing the problem, and if you are anything like me, that is sometimes the hardest thing to do.

What I see now, though, is that I have definitely experienced personal points in my life where I was anything but in the right frame of mind to want to improve professionally. I was too busy trying to convince myself that I was already a perfect educator to make myself feel better about not being a perfect human being. I think it is having this realization that is necessary for an educational leader to create the groundwork for a positive climate, and to then put into place whatever framework for quality professional development they wish to utilize. In other words, creating a culture that it is okay for all staff to know that realizing, acknowledging, and accepting that they are an imperfect person is the only way to begin the never-ending pursuit of becoming the closest thing to a perfect educator.

10

WHO WAS YOUR FAVORITE TEACHER GROWING UP?

*J*ust like a teacher has their favorite mini-lessons and anecdotal activities to use when they have a little extra time, so does an administrator when leading staff meetings. One of my favorite activities when discussing climate or culture is to simply ask everyone in the room to think of their favorite teacher without providing any more guidance or criteria than simply that.

I have posed this question to a variety of audiences. These include audiences such as a diverse building staff to a group of student-teachers all ready to embark on their new career. No matter the individual though, there are beautifully similar answers that I always get. Everyone responds by describing how their favorite teacher made them feel. They describe what their favorite teacher's personality was like. They describe how their favorite teacher's classroom was fun.

To this point, I have never had someone provide an answer about someone being their favorite teacher because of a specific instructional skill. This is something all educators need to examine and reflect upon. It seems as though almost all favorite teachers are determined by the climates they create rather than the instructional expertise they possess. Whether or not this should be this way though is moot in my mind. Instead, working towards determining what this means is paramount.

11

TEACHERS ARE SUPERHUMAN!

*W*hen I was growing up, like everyone else, I had my favorite teachers. It's fun to reflect because I have no doubt that every current educator has a similar past experience. They have those individuals that made learning amazing, made an impact, and made their students want to even perhaps envision themselves as a teacher in the future with their very own classroom.

However, what I think educators forget as their career evolves and continues is just how the students they have truly see them. Teachers are seen by the children they work with as a pseudo superhuman that is larger than life. It is a big deal when a child sees a teacher they adore out at a restaurant, gas station, or anywhere out of the ordinary within a community. Whenever someone imagines a famous movie star, we connect their existence to the platform they are most known for. For example, if an actor is well known as a character in a movie, we will naturally remember them as that character. It is really no different when a student sees a beloved teacher somewhere outside of their classroom.

These types of perceptions that students have of their teachers may be generally well known and accepted as the truth in students' minds. However, I also think educators that work to impact children do not necessarily forget this. Instead, I think they get used to it. While simply becoming accustomed to something by human nature, we have to remember that it is never that way for the students that love an educator. Even if a well-beloved teacher is used to students approaching them excitedly outside of school, an encounter will almost always be a big deal to a child.

STUDENTS DO NOT CARE WHAT A TEACHER'S EVALUATION SCORE IS

*T*he longer I am a school district administrator, the more I see many issues come up related to teacher evaluations. While I understand evaluation methods evolve and each state is different, no matter what the tool, they all will involve a summative designation in which a teacher is assigned a performance score. The consistent issue I then see is that the final summative designation is the only thing that seems to matter to an evaluatee. An evaluatee isn't interested in the feedback or ideas to improve. Instead, the ideal experience of an evaluation is based upon a score that signifies falsely that they are perfect.

Within whatever performance evaluation system someone is thinking of, we work in a field in which teachers spend so much time conducting their craft on their own that it becomes understandable for some to never really think that anyone else can truly be able to assess anything that they do. While this topic may have varying viewpoints, and be a catalyst for argument and debate, it may be best to acknowledge how little students actually care about what the actual score ends up being. I am sure some instances and examples will prove me wrong, but I have yet to truly see the evaluation score of a teacher affect how a student sees them. If a student adores a teacher, then they will not mind if their evaluation honestly lists areas that they could improve upon with professional development.

An evaluation becomes meaningless or a source of stress if there is no objectivity when identifying areas of growth. All of us have areas needing improvement, but some administrators are scared to document as such and some teachers are anything but receptive to hear it either. This is a systematic problem that is not easy to instantly fix, but school staff have to be working towards this being addressed if any professional development will have the impact that it could. If everyone's evaluation already says they are perfect, where is the need to change through guided improvement? Perhaps most importantly, can a teacher ever truly be at the "Action Level" of addressing social injustices if they are anything less than receptive to performance feedback?

13

THE MYTH OF THE PERFECT TEACHER

*B*eing a professional educator brings with it a challenge and demand that is unlike any other field. Professional educators work with students, and this makes the stakes unique and unmatched. If a child experiences only high-quality teachers and schools, it is impossible to even begin to equate how much more of a positive impact that it will have on the future of their life. In turn, the same assumption can easily be made when a child, unfortunately, experiences the opposite. Poor teachers and schools will only compound the challenge of life for children, and this is something that is obvious to conclude.

However, it is this overarching understanding that creates the unspoken norm in this field. No educator wants to admit they are anything but perfect. People have a hard time admitting their faults, and this trait is only compounded in the area of public education. Educators are not dealing with a product, sales quote, or monthly financial goal. Instead, they are dealing with children's lives, and with stakes that high, who wants to admit they are anything but the best?

Every professional field comes with expectations and pressure. However, the field of education is unique in that the professional development that is offered is sometimes resisted by the educators it is only meant to help. We can all recall instances in which these comments ring true. While each school and district is distinct, they all have days allocated for training and services aimed at making the educators that are a part of their team only better. While future parts of this book will outline and identify ways to ensure the professional development is high quality and purposeful, it is this brief section that aims to point out there is a deeper reason educators resist training intended to make them actually improve.

There is a myth in the education field shared by some that professional development is not necessary. In other words, there is a misconception that educators are already masters of their craft and simply have already reached the pinnacle of necessary skill. While reading it put this way it may seem unrealistic, I firmly believe this belief exists.

Some people think this is happening because there are some educators that are just not receptive to improving themselves. While there very well may be some of these types of educators, I instead think this is driven by educators not wanting to admit they have such a high stakes profession. A profession that is based upon being tasked to improve the lives of kids, and with this level of expectation, a fear for any educator to ever admit they are not perfect. Admitting as much, or even worse, admitting other educators are better than you creates rhetorical questions of self-doubt that are hard to embrace.

14

THE IMPLICATIONS OF DECLINISM
ON PUBLIC EDUCATION

*E*verywhere I have ever been as an educator, at some point, and in some way, I have heard the explanation that something used to be done a different way in the past, and that way was better. I always found this phenomenon fascinating. Why do some individuals become convinced that a point in the past will always be better than any possible future that could be embraced as time goes on? While I initially thought that this type of view was random, I have concluded that I believe it is instead related to the psychological concept of declinism.

The term declinism refers to the practice of some individuals creating beliefs within themselves that situations or issues were better in the past than they actually were. Considering the concept of declinism with education and professional development creates an interesting relationship to contemplate. Reflect on the topic of school safety for example. Lockdown emergency drills have become the norm, and preparing for a school shooting has become something that all district administrators focus upon. However, a perception that schools never had to prepare for catastrophic situations like these previously is simply not accurate.

Has anyone besides me ever heard someone make a comment that schools never had to prepare for unthinkable emergency situations before? During the 1950s, students were subjected to safety drills that involved them ducking and covering to prepare for the threat of a possible nuclear missile attack. It is just not accurate that public schools have never had to embrace being prepared for potentially disastrous situations (Archer, 2017).

Now consider the topic of declinism when focusing on improving instruction through professional development. There is established research that demonstrates which specific instructional strategies correlate to student achievement and also which do not (Marzano, 2001). This information exists and is accessible to educators, but it is not universally utilized.

A primary characteristic of declinism is ignoring the signs of improvement. Educators who have this viewpoint will confuse and ignore the growing pains associated with change, and the traits of implementation dips. In other words, declinism misses the assumption through ignorance or avoidance that an old practice might be blocking a new, more productive practice for improvement (Adelman, 2018).

Declinism is the idea that human beings are predisposed to view the past more favorably than the present and future. During the early 1990s, a phenomenon known as the "reminiscence" bump came to fruition. This research discovered that when elderly individuals were asked to recall their best or fondest memories, they typically best-remembered events that happened to them around the ages of 10 to 30 years of age (Etchells, 2015). Take that simple statement and then apply it to every professional development opportunity that just did not take hold with a teacher when it should have. Do educators only improve when they are also at their happiest and best place personally? At a minimum, is this concept important for educational leaders to realize when working to improve others? I think the answer is yes to both of these questions.

15

HOW DOES SELF-CARE IMPACT AN EDUCATOR'S ABILITY TO IMPROVE?

$\mathcal{O}$f all of the points I am most fearful in this booking rubbing people the wrong way, this small section of the book may be it. No public educator will be their best if they are not healthy. This state-ment is not based upon me claiming I have physical fitness, or life for that matter, more figured out than anyone else. However, being in a good place with your health through exercise is a topic that I think everyone deep down already inherently knows. The issue though is that if you are not at your best place physically, then the last thing anyone wants is for someone else to remind them of that.

Thus far in this book, I examined perhaps more easily accepted reasons educators may resist professional development. These included the myth of the perfect teacher and the concept of declinism. Both of the concepts result in individuals resisting the need to improve. However, not being at your best physically is different. It is different in that most people in poor health realize it. Instead, being in that state just causes them to be anything but receptive to possibly wanting to take those first (and most difficult) initial steps for improvement within any other part of their life.

Anyone that may doubt this point, or not see the correlation, should honestly reflect within their own life at their healthiest and unhealthiest times. I really don't think anyone needs to take the time to do research to support the claim I am trying to make either. All someone needs to do to examine and validate my point is to simply pick a morning to exercise before work and then pick another morning not to. The morning you begin with a workout, you will likely be in a better mood and more receptive to challenges that present themselves. The more an educator is both mentally and physically at their best, the more receptive they will be to improving themselves professionally.

Summary

First, we as a field have to rethink how we see teacher evaluations and all of the perceptions that come with them. If some people in the education field think they are already perfect, and they don't need any feedback, then any professional development ever offered will be pointless.

I think the answer to addressing this begins with everyone's memories of their own teachers growing up. Whether they were positive or negative experiences, they leave an impression that the teacher is a larger-than-life individual that is capable of anything. If you ask for someone to reflect on their favorite teachers growing up, they can easily conjure up reasons why they have chosen the persons that they did. However, when asking a group of individuals to do this, I have observed that many times the responses are more than simply quantifying specific instances on why they adored an educator. Instead, they have correlational relationships to how the former teacher was seen and made others feel. In some cases, this person had almost superhuman characteristics. In other words, many people's favorite teacher growing up was "perfect" and many people also believe that "education is just not as good as it used to be."

Why is there a tendency for people to think things were better at some point in the past than they are now? Does this tendency then affect current educators that need to continually improve themselves now, as well? And most importantly, if an educator is at a point in their life presently that they are far from their happiest personally, are they even in a frame of mind that they can improve professionally? Is this why every district has those "certain teachers" that hate every professional development opportunity—no matter how important and how it is presented?

SECTION 3: WHAT DOES THE RESEARCH INDICATE WHEN BUILDING PROFESSIONAL DEVELOPMENT PLANS?

While I have my own opinions on how to positively affect public education and benefit kids, I also try to do my best to have my decisions as an administrator be predominantly based upon research. I know there will always be a debate on whether or not teaching is an art or a science. Although I am tempted to select a position on this argument, I think it is far more important to acknowledge that our field does have research

that exists for any area that one can think of. How a school district should implement and build a professional development plan needs to be based upon addressing areas of growth, data, and most importantly research. If teachers should instruct based upon what the research indicates, and administrators are supposed to lead based upon what the research indicates, then professional development plans should also be no different.

NOT EVERYONE TAKES PROFESSIONAL DEVELOPMENT AND IMPROVEMENT SERIOUSLY

*O*ne of my first memories that were solidified in my mind as a beginning teacher was walking into a large auditorium with all of the teachers in a district. To say I felt nervous was an understatement. At this point in time, there was no such thing as a teacher shortage and any premise of such would have seemed unheard of. Getting my first job was competitive, so walking into my first position was exciting, but also nerve-racking. I had both ambition and fear that I needed to make sure that I did well enough that the last four years of my life as an undergraduate majoring in elementary education wasn't all for naught.

I envisioned the start of the year of the school where educators were intent professionals excited and determined to discuss pedagogy to further grow when compared to the year before. There were some educators that did indeed fit this profile; however, to my utter shock and horror was the realization that this was not the norm for everyone. Instead, I found a small portion of teachers that saw the beginning-of-the-year faculty institute as an opportunity to do anything but try to improve from the previous year. I saw teachers that were indifferent and uninterested. I saw teachers that were definitely in the "Indifference Level" of my social justice assessment. However, most sad, as I truly reflect, is that there eventually were times I fell into this trap of consensual negativity when experiencing lackluster professional development attempts.

I am a very concrete sequential person that craves clear and distinct directions on ideas to improve as an educator. I want to know what the research indicates, and have a difficult time with only opinions not based on facts when discussing these types of topics. However, my personality both personally and professionally is certainly not necessarily the ideal either, or the norm. I have, though, reached a point where I feel comfortable making the following summarizing comment. I do not understand why so many educational institutions think some type of "one and done" keynote speaker, who does not include specific strategies for improvement with zero follow-through, are going to have a positive impact. Why do we as educators work in a field in which we think professional development, that is not foundational upon improving instruction through some type of long-term commitment, is worthwhile or beneficial?

"ONE AND DONE KEYNOTES" OR PROFESSIONAL TRAINERS? THERE IS A DIFFERENCE!

*R*ecently, my car broke down to the point it needed a repair by someone much more educated than myself about auto repair. I take pride, and try very hard, to fix various items and issues myself in my personal life (even though many times I just end up making the issue worse). This necessary repair was something far beyond my limited scope of expertise. To put it bluntly, I did not know how to repair my car myself, and it entirely was this way because I did not have the knowledge or skill set to do so. In turn, my inability to fix my car had nothing to do with me needing a more positive attitude to be able to.

I have attended and listened to so many keynotes during my professional career that I have noticed a trend. So many of these individuals seem to adhere to the same format that basically consists of the following:

- *Summarize to the audience a difficult situation that they encountered or a challenge they overcame*
- *Describing how this instance elicited a change in their professional and/or personal life*
- *Including pictures displaying some of the changes they made in a fun and playful manner*

- *Encouraging others to overcome adversity through a positive mindset of some kind*

In turn, I have attended some great keynote speakers, and this in no way is meant to belittle or negatively describe any and all of them. Obviously, like any other profession, some keynote speakers are better than others, and as such, some are fantastic. However, the ones that strictly follow the format listed above do so little, if anything, to indicate how exactly someone is supposed to actually improve or change.

I could listen to a variety of keynote speakers on auto repair, and the ones with only a positive message would not help me at all. If I do not know how to do the actual repair, then a positive message does not change that. This is the analogy that I want to make within public education. So many educators attend keynote speaking sessions, and I think they have this same experience. They have an issue or a challenge that they want to find potential answers on how to fix, but unfortunately, they instead are only given a motivational speech alluding to a premise that more positivity will somehow fix the issue itself.

To be frank, I don't think enough keynote speakers working with educators realize this either. The vast majority of all teachers and administrators are wonderful, hardworking people that need solutions specific to instructional strategies. In other words, they want and need to be specifically told how to "repair their car." I think educational leaders also need to begin questioning why keynote speakers are even used during seminars, workshops, and institute days almost to the point that it seems automatic in many settings.

Within the field of public education, there are frequently times in which we all hear anecdotal stories on why and how a school improved. These stories may or may not be embellished, but they so often involve a dramatic improvement through a new program, new leader, new building, etc. Personally, in turn, I have never heard of an instance of dramatic improvement occurring because a school district had just brought in a particular keynote speaker. Significant improvement comes from more than just a one-time presentation.

WHY SHOULD EDUCATORS BE AWARE OF DEWEY, PIAGET, AND VYGOTSKY?

*J*n many ways, the answer to this question is truly simplistic. No matter what your position in the education field, you need to have values and goals whose premises are built upon credibility. When values and goals are simply opinions, they have no true substance and it makes people naturally question the notion. However, when values and goals are based upon established and widely accepted research it brings objectivity.

Establishing credibility can be a complex topic to address. Having a solution or idea that everyone else believes is not an easy thing. It takes more than the right answer. It also takes charisma, rapport, and maybe even a little luck. However, having a true base understanding of not only what quality instruction is, but also how it is known to be makes convincing others that much easier.

UNDERSTANDING JOHN DEWEY'S PERSPECTIVE ON CURRICULUM AND INSTRUCTION

I can definitely remember being an overwhelmed undergraduate student trying to balance homework assignments, working part-time to afford to be able to go to school, and also trying to have some type of personal life. When I eventually got to the courses that addressed instructional methods though, I am not sure if the impression that should have been left upon me happened. Interestingly, this lack of impression might have also been partly my own fault. I was probably too driven by completing an assignment to get a good grade than progressing with a mindset that learning this information would be necessary for my success as a future instructional leader.

Most educators today have heard suggestions on making instruction for students inquiry-based and that curriculum should be driven at least somewhat by student interest. So many educators have general ideas of what teachers should do based upon evaluation frameworks like Charlotte Danielson's, but I am not sure how many know the historical research that stems from these frameworks through today. Long before any current educational trainer now, John Dewey was advocating for fewer classrooms built upon rote memorization and more built upon making education an experience led by the very child themselves. While deeply understanding many of Dewey's views would make an educator a better leader for improving others through professional development, I think most educators have at least heard of this individual. However, I am unsure to what extent they are familiar. Similar to how I think "one and done keynotes" is only scratching at the surface of improvement, I also see the true value of having at least a basic understanding of the historical foundations of educational research to then help others understand the evolution of instructional practices.

In 1894, the Dewey family moved to Chicago, Illinois, and enrolled their children at the school of Cook County Normal and were influenced enough by what they saw that they decided to establish their own laboratory school in 1896. The goal of the new institution was to implement Dewey's theories and their effects on society. The school continued until 1904 when Dewey left for Columbia, but its impact during this brief period of time should not be underestimated. This venture is credited with creating substantial excitement within the country as it was seen as firsthand evidence of education progressing towards a new and improved reality (Cremlin, 1961; Thomas, 1962).

The purpose of the laboratory school, as Dewey described, was to discover the best practices through hands-on implementation of methods of learning, teaching, and discipline. In addition, there were goals to explore the most impactful manners for a school to become a cooperative community, while also developing students into the best versions of themselves as an individual. Dewey further describes the overall purpose of life itself as being foundational upon educational experience and that learning should be a by-product of social activity (Cremlin, 1961; Thomas, 1962). It becomes fascinating to me that even at this point in history, educational researchers realized that educating a child as a whole was necessary, and addressing social-emotional needs was important. These types of topics are anything but new, but only may be new to a teacher that has not received this type of professional development. Helping to provide the context that so many ideas today have existed and been advocated for decades before assists with the inevitable challenge of buy-in when recommending a change.

Unfortunately, the existence and creation of Dewey's school ended up not having the success and attention many would assume. Instead, it was the perspective and approach on curriculum that created broad, societal interest. Up until this point in education, Dewey felt that the main subject areas were not being taught in any kind of cohesive manner. He believed they should be presented to students with symmetry and that educational experiences should be synonymous with the human experience. He advocated for a child's natural interests and curiosity to be taken into account when constructing a course of study, and this was in many ways a sharp contrast to the norms of public education at the time (Dewey, 1916; Kliebard, 2004).

As Dewey's perspectives on curriculum became a catalyst for this time in education, it was also met with the rise of social efficiency. While Dewey concentrated on a curriculum based upon scientific inquiry for individual realization, the pioneers for social efficiency wanted to see a much different approach. Specifically, this viewpoint takes the stance that the scope of a school's curriculum needed to be broadened beyond only intelligence acquisition. It needed to also include the intangibles within life activities and soft skills such as teamwork, problem-solving, or time-management (Dewey, 1916; Kliebard, 2004).

Even though Dewey's curriculum was based upon an approach of somewhat precise standards, advocates of social efficiency saw this as a point in history when certain social institutions, such as church and family, were beginning to decline and that schools needed to be restructured to make up for this difference. Social efficiency proponent Franklin Bobbit had the perspective that ultimately no curriculum could truly encompass all the information involved within human activity. However, he understood that some information will be learned through direct and intended inclusion, and other pieces of information will be discovered inadvertently (Dewey, 1916; Kliebard, 2004).

There are obvious differences between the Dewey perspective on curriculum and with social efficiency educators. Dewey ultimately did not see a curriculum as a means to prepare individuals for concise steps in a process of learning outcomes. He saw education as a means to capitalize on natural curiosity and self-interest as individuals strive to learn more about themselves and the world they live in (Dewey, 1916; Kliebard, 2004). Dewey saw the value of ensuring learning took place in a real-world and practical setting. He very much rejected the practice of instructional strategies that include repetitive, rote memorization methods of instruction, and instead championed approaches that required students to be engulfed in real-world learning scenarios. These approaches should be entwined with collaboration so that knowledge and learning can elicit student creativity through opportunities for peer inter-action. (Hickman, Reich, & Neubert, 2013).

Dewey rejected the dualistic epistemology that subject matter and methodology are two totally separate affairs in education. This idea can be described as seeing content as an existing collection of itemized facts and principles about both the world and us as human beings. In turn, then the instruction is simply the chosen manner in which to best facilitate the acquisition of this information for hopeful long-term possession (Dewey, 1916). Dewey's position on the relationship between subject matter and method is applicable still to this day. He argued that instructional strate-gies used are not a standalone separate from content, but instead, instruc-tional methods should be an arrangement of the subject matter itself. Dewey's (1916) position is well described below.

In theory, at least, one might deduce from a science of the mind as something existing by itself a complete theory of methods of learning, with no knowledge of the subjects to which they are to be applied. Since many who are actually most proficient in various branches of subject matter are wholly innocent of these methods, this state of affairs gives an opportunity for the retort that pedagogy, as an alleged science of methods of the mind in learning, is futile. It is a mere screen for concealing the necessity that a teacher is of profound and accurate acquaintance with the subject in hand.

But since thinking is a directed movement of subject matter to a completing issue, and since mind is the deliberate and intentional phase of the process of any such split is radically false. The fact that the material of a science is organized is evidence that it has already been subjected to intelligence; it has been methodized, so to say. Zoology as a systematic branch of knowledge represents crude, scattered facts of our ordinary acquaintance with animals after they have been subjected to careful examination, deliberate supplementation, and to an arrangement to bring out connections which assist observation, memory, and further inquiry. Instead of furnishing a starting point for learning, they mark out a consummation. Method means that arrangement of subject matter which makes it most effective in use. Never is method something outside of the material. (pp. 164-165)

Whether an educator reading this book is hoping to improve because they are receiving or leading professional development, it is powerful to realize that historical educational figures like John Dewey have been advocating that instruction should be based upon true experiences and not memorization of facts. Understanding and being able to articulate that this position is anything but new will make its implementation that much easier to justify now.

SO WHAT IS COLLABORATIVE LEARNING EXACTLY?

"*J*ust know good teaching when I see it." I have heard that phrase, or something very similar to it, more than a few times from administrators when discussing the topic of evaluation. Honestly, it always makes me grimace when I hear this type of comment. I feel like this type of perception among some evaluators makes the challenge of improving educators through professional development difficult when they take so little interest in basing feedback upon actual best practice research. However, if the phrase "good teaching" is meant to be synonymous with student achievement through instructional practices, then the term many are referring to, whether or not they realize it, would be constructivism.

Having a base understanding of the term constructivism is important whether you are an educational administrator, teacher, or anything else in between. It defines experience-based learning and is important when either building quality professional development or being able to identify effective teaching. So many modern perspectives on best practice instructional approaches today are derived from this concept, and the work of Jean Piaget is widely accepted as the foundation of constructivism.

Piaget posited that individuals learn based upon experiences, active exploration of their environment, and the process of equilibration, or making sense of new learning (Piaget & Inhelder, 1969). Piaget described this as occurring through accommodation and assimilation. Assimilation is when a learner takes new information and builds a relationship with it into older, prior experiences. It expands an already existing schema. Accommodation, on the other hand, is when a learner takes new information and reframes it because what they just learned did not operate within the manner or context that was expected. The creation of a new schema is often required. These two avenues depend on the individual taking in information and then actively incorporating it into their mind as an individualistic inception, producing knowledge and meaning based upon their own experiences (Glaserfeld, n.d.; Piaget, 1978; Piaget, Smith & Brown, 2011).

Piaget's theory of learning often contradicts the assumption many teachers hold on how to teach and on how learners learn. The position that a teacher's role is to simply instill information upon students has traditionally been held by society and teachers as shown through the way our system of education has evolved. Piaget's research has defined learning as best occurring when led by the students, while the teacher is a facilitator of the process. This evolution on how to create successful classrooms is then a catalyst for instructional strategies to create environments conducive to student-led learning (Glaserfeld, n.d.; Piaget, 1978; Piaget, Smith & Brown, 2011).

Dewey advocated for experience-based learning. Piaget established constructivism. And then Lev Vygotsky took this area of work a step further to define true collaborative learning. This triad of concepts is all based upon the type of instruction all schools should strive for to garner not only student engagement but also achievement.

Lev Vygotsky was a constructivist whose work was prominent shortly after Piaget's. Vygotsky proposed that the learning and development of new skills occur through collaborative activities (Vygotsky, Cole, Stein & Sekula, 1978). Similar to Piaget, his research concluded that learning must be personal and based upon experiences. However, he believed that new learning was very much affected by the context of social characteristics such as culture, history, religion, and traditions.

Vygotsky concluded that for learning to occur, an individual will first make contact with the new concept on an interpersonal level but will then internalize the concept on a personal level (Kozulin, 2007; Vygotsky, Davidov & Silverman, 1997).

Vygotsky's view on constructivism is specifically referred to as social constructivism. The concept of the zone of proximal development is a foundational aspect of his theory. This is the distance between an individual's actual level of development and the level an individual could potentially reach. He believed that this possible cognitive development is limited in many ways to the chronological age of the specific individual. However, educators can help guide this acquisition of new skills by incorporating hands-on learning activities that allow for connections to past experiences (Kozulin, 2007). The role of the teacher in facilitating this learning is to provide scaffolding, in other words, the appropriate assistance to help the learners achieve what they cannot do yet on their own (Vygotsky, Cole, Stein & Sekula, 1978; Vygotsky, Davidov & Silverman, 1997).

STRATEGIC PLANS - WHERE IS THE EMPHASIS ON IMPROVING INSTRUCTION?

*T*he longer I am in this field, the more I see similarities that are universal for every school and district that I definitely do not think are positive. Specifically, almost every district will have a school board that creates some type of strategic plan that is then proudly placed on the district's website. Not to sound critical, but I would challenge any educator reading this book at this point to go to their own district's website, and I can just about guarantee that I can predict the general outline for the strategic plan that is on there.

The strategic plan will have the general outline described below:

- *Student Achievement*
- *Building Infrastructure*
- *Finances*
- *Community Relations*

Now just like each school district will have its own unique traits and qualities, each district will also have its own style and approach to a strategic plan. Regardless though, there has become this unspoken and unacknowledged norm that the four items listed above will be included.

Even though just listing them accomplishes nothing, everyone seems to feel better by doing so.

I feel so strongly that this practice is useless, and at worse harmful, that I think an entire book could be published simply examining this perspective. The field of education is a beautiful field because there is no such thing as a finish line, and the work of researchers discussed previously seems to certainly support this. There is never a point in which a school has reached a utopian phase of perfection that there isn't work left to be done. Due to this continual state of potential and necessary improvement, there will always be room for growth.

Another way of considering the point I am trying to make is how these four continually used themes of strategic plans are all aspects of a school that should have no finish line. Consider the topic of community relations. Is there ever a time that a school shouldn't have this be a focus for improvement? Or more importantly, is there ever a time that a school has reached a point of having this target somehow accomplished?

I think a funny thing happens when the strategic plans take this generic and safe approach. They create superficial comfort that a district is tackling important issues that all stakeholders quickly analyzing the direction of a district will find satisfactory, but they are non-specific enough that it doesn't create any actual change. Almost every person, educator or not, knows what it entails to make a new year's resolution. While the goals that are involved with this type of experience are obviously vastly different based upon each person, similar to a school district, there are goals that are also applicable to all people. These could perhaps include being financially stable, having satisfying personal relationships, and being physically healthy.

These generic types of goals that many districts utilize have the same approach that is used by many with personal goals for improvement. The goals are the types that should always be areas of focus regardless. A school district always needs to have an emphasis on student achievement, building infrastructure, finances, and community relations. In turn, for example, every person in the world knows that they need to be healthy to be at their best, so do they really find any benefit by establishing that they need to do something that is so obvious? Is there any person that truly doesn't understand already that they want to continually and ideally be a better version of themselves?

For any strategic plan, whether it is for a school district, individual person, or whatever else, it is only worthwhile if the plan has actual substance. Now to me, substance is defined by objectivity through an actual target. Using weight loss as an example, wouldn't there be a lot more purpose behind a strategic plan that said, "I will lose 20 pounds by running 2 miles every day," rather than simply "I will be healthy."? Imagine if this same approach was used by school districts, and how then the professional development created to address goals would be so much more purposeful.

COMPLIANCE IS NOT ENGAGEMENT

I think whenever someone begins talking about quality instruction and what exactly that it is, it is necessary to begin with a discussion on how someone actually defines quality instruction. It has taken me working in this field for a while to really understand varying interpretations of this concept, and why sometimes eliciting discussions about instruction many times are anything but productive. Quality instruction is not always interpreted by all educators as practices that connect to student engagement, and I am not entirely sure why that is that way.

Instead, some educators define quality instruction as having a classroom full of compliant students. A compliant student is one that takes all directions from the teacher, does not talk unless absolutely necessary, and is a recipient of all learning while not taking the lead for any of their knowledge acquisition directly. A compliant student may appear that they are retaining new information, but the primary variable they demonstrate is being quiet above all else.

It is not my purpose to state that student compliance isn't a necessary aspect for success in a classroom. However, I am saying that student compliance does not always connect to student learning. This is a really important concept to articulate because if I want to describe how and why instruction matters, not having a collective definition of what quality instruction is would make that virtually impossible.

LECTURING IS NOT THE ONLY TYPE
OF INSTRUCTIONAL STRATEGY

*M*y definition of quality instruction is that it must correlate to student engagement, and there is a lot of research that supports this. Engagement is not necessarily compliance. However, it is so important to acknowledge that teachers that only lecture are only utilizing one type of instructional strategy, and not a very good one at that. In turn, lecturing is not a completely bad instructional strategy either. It can be valuable as a means of classroom communication, and it is definitely a necessary component of a teacher's arsenal to instill learning.

The key is an understanding that lecturing cannot and should not be the predominant approach for any educator. Obviously having content knowledge is paramount, but if effective teaching was just explaining content through lecture then anyone could be a successful teacher. I have encountered teachers absolutely in love with their content, and there is certainly nothing wrong with that. However, the best teachers will also love instruction, and most importantly, understand that lecturing is not the only type.

Whenever someone imagines a boring teacher, they imagine someone that does nothing but lecture to a class of students. While this statement may seem overly simplified, it is an important one to make. An ineffective teacher only lectures, and even though this is obviously my opinion, this statement is also absolutely dominated through support of the research on constructivism outlined earlier in the book. If students are simply receiving information, this is not enough. They must be applying newly learned information. Learning has to be conceptual and hands-on, and at this point in our society, there is also no excuse for anything other than that in a classroom.

Classrooms based upon rote memorization through lecture needs to stop. If a piece of information is an item that any student can simply google, then why is the teacher wasting time teaching it? Instruction has to align to strategies and approaches that allow for learning to be guided by the learner, and in turn, so should professional development.

Summary

I truly do not think enough educators engage in significant and ongoing discussions about the topic of instruction. Not enough educators have a complete understanding on the impact of educational pioneers such as John Dewey. While I am the first to acknowledge that having an intense historical knowledge of the evolution of public education is certainly not necessary for a successful teacher, having a basic understanding definitely does not hurt. How educators define good instruction is vastly different, and I am convinced this is a large issue facing our field today. To best establish a universally accepted definition, I believe basing it upon widely accepted research is a way that needs to be considered.

Outside of a very very small few, all educators that enter the field do so with a genuine passion to want to help kids. However, if when they were a student themselves if all they were exposed to were teachers that predominantly lectured, it is possible that this could then lead to all that they do, as well. We have to ensure teachers understand the concept of constructivism and create professional development plans that are based on this.

The answers for increased student success exist in the research.

However, before one educator can convince another to change, they simply have to have an understanding of the most impactful types of instruction. Sometimes the hard part is not so much identifying the problem. Instead, it is convincing others that their answer to a solution just may not be the correct answer after all.

SECTION 4: UNDERSTANDING AND APPLYING A PROFESSIONAL DEVELOPMENT PLAN OUTLINE

I think anything good in life has to have a plan. Now don't get me wrong. Part of the beauty in life is the randomness that also makes it beautiful. However, I am an individual that believes someone who depends entirely too much on luck will probably never see the success

that they could have. Quality professional development that impacts and improves instruction for the benefit of students will not just magically happen. It has to be implemented through a plan, and this chapter provides that plan. There are four parts of this implementation, and this section of the book is aimed to help any educator be able to ensure their professional development has the impact that they are hoping for.

24

THERE IS NO SILVER BULLET

*B*efore I can begin describing the ideal professional development outline to make it meaningful, a few key points must be made. These points are necessary enough that if individuals skip past every part of this book to the outline at the end of this section, it will not have the value that it could.

To begin with, I am not an individual claiming that my idea is the perfect solution for all issues within public education. In fact, I believe that there are already individuals that are claiming to have this type of secret and sought-after solution for any problem found in schools. Ironically enough, I think that this approach is actually one of the largest issues in this field. There is no perfect answer, but the outline I describe is a blueprint for a process. I use the terms blueprint and process very purposefully because they imply necessary modifications may be needed based on the potential school or district they are being utilized within. This understanding is necessary because there are too many endlessly manipulated variables to ever claim there is an idea that is ideal for each school, and anyone that claims they have one should make you concerned.

Next, this outline is a combination of my personal experiences, research involved with my dissertation, and most importantly, networking and learning from my peers in this field. As an educational leader, one universal truth that I have uncovered is that every good thing that I have ever been involved with, or accomplished, involved others. For example, if there was ever a particularly successful school initiative or program that I led, it involved the input from other staff. In addition, if there was ever a particularly successful recommendation I made at the school board level, it involved the advice and input from the board members, community stakeholders, and even other educational leaders in other districts. My point being, the best ideas are driven and evolved by many and not a few.

One of the most beautiful parts of life is the unpredictability of it. I am a procedure-driven person that loves order and predictability. However, life is just not that way. I bring this up because this outline should be viewed through that lens. It is not something that any one individual should try to utilize through a rigid and individualized approach. Instead, it should be a guide for many when they work towards the never-ending pursuit of improvement for the specific student body they aim to serve.

25

QUALITY PROFESSIONAL DEVELOPMENT DESCRIPTOR #1 – HAVE AN OBJECTIVE GOAL

*E*arlier in this book, I addressed the inappropriate tendency with districts to create super subjective goals in their strategic plans. At this point, I want to take this a step further. To begin, I want everyone to think for a few moments about the last couple of initiatives that they witnessed their school or district implement. There will undoubtedly be exceptions, but I will challenge everyone to now ask themselves if the new initiatives also had predetermined and objective targets that they were aware of, and at a later time, was it determined if the new initiative also had a positive impact supported through data.

For example, at this time in education, there are many districts that are providing teachers and students with more and more items of technology to use in the classroom. Whether it is tablets in the pre-school classrooms, interactive whiteboards in a middle school classroom, or laptops for every child at a high school, it is happening in many places. To be pithy with my own viewpoint on technology, I do think it is a necessary and unmatched resource that should be in every classroom. Technological access creates a ubiquitous atmosphere of inquiry that computers with internet access can certainly help to provide. However, how many districts have no predetermined target, or even idea, of how they will decide if the implementation of any such resource was successful?

Recently, I remember seeing district after district institute one-to-one computer programs under the guise that this would easily and instantly solve whatever issue they had. I think this misguided approach is based upon no one ever demanding that there be intended results, and also because, frankly, it is easy to move forward when there is no way to determine success. With whatever issue or challenge a district has, it feels good and provides a premade response that giving all students laptops would correlate to student achievement. However, what I began to see when I would directly ask districts a year or two later how it was going after their computer program implementations, the response I would essentially get would entail, "It went great! It was awesome!" While these types of answers, also accompanied by plenty of social media posts of students using laptops in seemingly engaging ways, were enough to appease many, they were not enough to appease me. There was no data. There was no substance.

In my mind, I would assume that a district that had spent hundreds of thousands of dollars on technology resources would want, if not require, more of a targeted approach to determine if something was worthwhile. Why it is that way somewhat fascinates me. Without a targeted goal, there is no manner to determine at a later date that the professional development was successful, and without this, it destroys future credibility that professional development will always be worthwhile.

Below is what I would consider to be a straightforward, objective, and accountability driven goal. The format provides the strategy being implemented, a timeline for success, and the target. This does not have to be complicated, and the worse goal is the one that doesn't exist. *"Student performance at the end of the school year , as determined by state assessments, will increase by 3% as a contributing result of the Webb's Depth of Knowledge training for teachers."* This simple goal can be advertised, and it allows for there to be a determination if the practice that was implemented had an intended result.

THE CHANGE PROCESS

*C*hange is necessary, and most understand this reality no matter the field one finds themselves in. The world is always changing, and because of that, moving forward becomes synonymous with continually embracing new challenges. While I understand the stress affiliated with change, I think it sometimes goes badly not because of the new solution that is being proposed. Instead, it is because there was never an established purpose on why to change in the first place.

The reason the topic of change needs to be connected to building quality professional development is that whatever training is being considered has to demonstrate an alignment as a solution to fix a problem. Although this statement may seem obvious, it is not the consistent norm for professional development many times.

I personally witness so many individuals that build district- or building-level professional development plans that are completely random in nature. I sometimes encounter educational leaders that select professional development by whatever unsolicited email or letter they get offering some type of training. In other words, there are fads for professional development, and while some fads may become popular because of value, they should not be the predominant reason they are selected.

There needs to be a shift on how educators define the change process. Change should not be seen as just the new "thing" that is being implemented. Instead, change needs to be seen as the new training aimed at solving a problem. When there is this difference in approach and perspective, change is done with fidelity and without as much fear.

QUALITY PROFESSIONAL DEVELOPMENT #2 – HAVE A LIST OF CURRICULAR ESSENTIAL SKILLS

*A*ll school districts need to have a quality curriculum. No one will deny that. No one questions that. No one will disagree with that. What I do find interesting is how different individual districts define curriculum. Examining these differences to establish a universal definition is important for the process of establishing quality professional development. So why is a list of curriculum essential skills important? The most basic and prolific answer to that question is how else will a teacher new to a school somehow know what to teach.

One of the schools I taught at was a warm and inviting junior high that had a lot of veteran teachers that were an honor to work with. Like most schools, they also had a mentoring program in which an experienced teacher would be paired with a new teacher to help them with all of the aspects of joining a new building that one could imagine. This included explaining the procedures for entering grades, specifics on the master schedule, and discussing which concepts of curriculum to teach and when.

It occurred to me years later as a principal leading professional development that this mentor teacher had full autonomy to decide what new teachers he worked with would teach. This individual could have told me anything in regards to curriculum expectations, and I would have probably followed it because I was a new teacher wanting to do well and please the veteran teachers whose team I was joining. Fortunately for me, this former mentor steered me in the right direction, but this could have not been the case.

Consider, for example, if the mentor teacher had created his own curriculum map of student milestones that was not aligned to state standards and was based on simply memorizing useless facts. Imagine if his curriculum had no expectations of students implementing skills through conceptual activities that aligned to the educational pioneers such as Dewey, Piaget, or Vygotsky. What if his entire curriculum inadvertently depended upon student behavioral compliance rather than mastery of content? If it had been, and I was agreeable to his positions on curriculum, would I have then instructed in a way that I would have depended entirely on lecturing information with the goal that students memorize what I say? In turn, would I have also been resistant to instructional professional development aimed at implementing conceptual instructional strategies?

Schools must have an established foundation of skills that students are taught at various milestones, and this pacing really should not be different despite new teachers coming and going. I am a large proponent of instructor autonomy, but this autonomy has to be placed correctly. Teachers need to provide input into what their curriculum is, but there also has to be a level of guidance that maps the skills that address higher-order thinking and pacing of content that ensures students learn all that they need to. Without having this, the task of ensuring quality instruction takes place through professional development is like building a house with the roof before the walls are in place.

CURRICULUM IS NOT A RESOURCE

$\mathcal{I}$t is important to define curriculum correctly for the purpose of this next step. However, since this is my view and interpretation, it does not necessarily mean that it is my goal to change your perspective if you have a different one. What I do feel is necessary is that there is no confusion about curriculum and a resource being seen as the same thing. Any type of confusion would be a significant block towards the improvement of instruction.

Curriculum should be a living document that simply identifies what tangible and demonstrable skills students should obtain at various points of their educational experience. It should be skills that are specific and are indicative of being conceptual in nature. What it should not be is a document that is a checklist of items that are dependent upon rote memorization, or even worse, an item that is actually a resource that is being used at a specific time. For example, if a district determined that a student "should be able to summarize varying viewpoints of a non-fiction…," this would be an ideal start of an essential skill for a quality curriculum. This type of approach allows autonomy of instruction and resource selection for the teacher, but also requires the necessary expectation of what skills should be taught and when by the district.

However, consider the inappropriateness of a curriculum that would include items such as "Students will memorize all of the state capitals," or "Students will read chapter 1 of their textbook." The first example is only rote memorization and requires zero higher-order thinking. The second example is a resource, and the reason this is dangerous is that the task depends on no teacher instruction. Merely exposing students to a resource does not align with student achievement.

TECHNOLOGY IS NOT AN
INSTRUCTIONAL STRATEGY

*J*ust as dangerous as misconceptions about a resource being a curriculum is the misconception that technology is an instructional strategy. I am the first to identify myself as an educator that loves technology, sees it as an unmatched necessity, and understands the power it has for unlimited student engagement. However, technology is a resource, and when educators start to think it is something other than that, instruction will be affected.

As discussed previously in this book, many in the field have implemented one-to-one laptop programs especially as districts deal with a pandemic they never anticipated. Now in my opinion, what began as a realization of some forward-thinking school districts that realized 21st-century learners need technology that is ubiquitous in a classroom has now evolved to a false notion that giving all kids school computers would be the answer to solve every issue in public education.

I can recall when the thought of all students being supplied computers seemed like a futuristic and exciting idea, but slowly the idea became a reality. However, a teacher that was seen as ineffective before an infusion of technology because of poor instructional skills does not magically become effective because every child has a tablet. Consider a teacher that was only lecturing while students took notes. This would be an ineffective teacher. Now consider a teacher that is utilizing a large video screen with lots of fancy clip art while all of the students take notes while typing on a laptop. Would this teacher be any more effective, even though they are using technology, despite the poor instructional strategies being utilized?

A teacher that is exemplary, but uses zero technology, is exemplary because of the instructional strategies that they implement. In turn, a teacher that is poor in practice, but a master of technological resources, does not instantly become more proficient. This simple truth is not only why technology is not an instructional strategy, but also why this misconception is dangerous.

A CURRICULUM BUILT ON ESSENTIAL SKILLS PROVIDES AUTONOMY

*A*ll schools and districts are different, and these differences are a positive thing because they help to establish universal truths. For example, one universal truth is students and staff will enjoy a well-timed snow day if they are fortunate enough to live in a region that has this type of inclement weather. While there are always exceptions to any overarching claim, I would be a hard person to convince that people don't enjoy learning they can sleep in at the last moment when they were anticipating a normal workday. Now consider this analogy through an instructional perspective. Does anyone know of any teachers that prefer being told exactly how to teach? That has definitely never been my experience.

Having a teacher coached and provided feedback will be a lot better received than having someone come into their classroom and tell them how exactly to instruct. Whether or not someone is an educator, people enjoy autonomy, and in my opinion, teachers want it as much as any profession. Based on this observation, I continue to be amazed when school district leaders attempt to implement curriculums that are rigid enough to encompass mandated instructional strategies that can even go as far as including scripted narratives.

Whenever I hear about a mandated curriculum that outlines not only what everyone should be doing to the week, day, and even minute, it requires a policing of teacher practice that should be a red flag to anyone that has common sense. This type of teaching staff will have a curriculum that will never be done with any fidelity. I just do not understand why anyone thinks this approach to curriculum will ever work long-term. These procedurally dictated curriculums usually begin with a heavy buy-in, which may or may not be forced, that will then falter as time goes on.

Consider, for example, if someone is bound and determined to get into better physical condition, and goes all-in with a very rigid outlined plan to improve themselves. Perhaps, for example, a person has decided that they are going to jog five miles every morning. Any person with reasonable sense would agree and realize that if someone jogs five miles every morning, this will create positive results. However, if the plan to jog five miles is not something sustainable, then who cares what the results could or even should be?

The key to curriculum is to make it into a list of autonomy-laden skills rather than a strict guideline that acts as a rigid blueprint. Using the jogging analogy above, I would encourage a person to simply decide that they were going to exercise each day rather than decide that they were going to jog a set amount at a predetermined time. This approach allows fluidity for the individual. They can make decisions to modify their approach based upon how they feel, the weather, or even if they just feel like running more than five miles.

Curriculum development needs to address which milestones students should meet that correlate to state standards and local district beliefs. An example of what I am implying would be the following.

" A student will be able to read a nonfiction article and summarize the main idea while determining the different points of view. "

This example of an essential skill is conceptual in nature. It allows for a student to apply skills and knowledge that they have obtained to demonstrate accomplishment of the goal. The manner in which this example is written does not dictate what nonfiction article will be used. It allows flexibility for the topic that the article would be about. However, the essential skill requires constructivist instruction, and most importantly, not a rote memorization approach. A curriculum should have three to five of these types of essential skills for each content area and grade level. It should include specific time periods that also provide succinct obtainment of knowledge at similar times for all students. This allows for the autonomy of resources and instructional approach for teachers.

An example of a curricular essential skill that is not appropriate would be the following.

A student will memorize and restate the causes of World War I.

While this example may seem obvious to the point I am trying to make, it is also necessary to point out that this is an actual example of a skill an educator I have worked with thought was sufficient. There is nothing higher-order or conceptual about a curriculum with this type of expectation, so it frankly bothers me that there are classrooms with these types of atmospheres. Even more dangerous though are curricular essential skills similar to the following.

"Chapter 1 – American History"

If a school or district lists various resources and implies that they are their curriculum, this is fraught with issues. A resource is not a replacement for instruction, and when a resource becomes synonymous with curriculum then it presumes that is all that is needed for a student to learn. If a textbook series is the answer, then students do not need to do anything besides read or listen to it to then learn. This resource-driven approach to curriculum also takes away the beautiful options of freedom for a teacher. If they are passionate about certain themes or topics within unit planning, they are not then able to engage in personal preferences if whatever specific resource they have to use is preselected for them.

This is why an approach to building curriculum through three to five essential skills by content and grade level for each grading period is an ideal approach. It is supported by research through a constructivist view of learning if the skills are conceptual in nature. It allows teacher autonomy on what instructional strategies to use. Lastly, it allows for an ever-changing usage of resources that should match student needs and interests.

31

WHAT SHOULD THE PROCESS BE TO BUILD A QUALITY CURRICULUM?

*N*ow at this point in this book, there have been undoubtedly several bold statements. However, I think the best educational leaders (and I am hopeful to one day be one in this category) make the occasional bold statements. Under this premise, I make the following comment with as much boldness as I can.

It should not take long to build a curriculum document of essential skills. It should not be a long undertaking involving countless committees, meetings, and endless debate. It could take as little as a day when all staff is available. The reason is that a curriculum of essential skills should be built upon the learning standards that a state provides for its public schools. It is when concepts such as unit themes, resources, or specific instructional strategies that *are not curriculum* begin to become (incorrectly) synonymous with content that this process becomes difficult or unsuccessful.

The key to creating this type of timeline is ensuring that all teachers of the same grade levels and content areas understand the expectation that this just needs to be three to five essential skills for each of the four grading periods, and these skills are only identifying the when and how all of the mandated learning standards will be addressed. Once this is universally understood, the next step is creating the understanding that this document is not one that is ever finished. I have seen, and believe, many teachers become frozen to ever commit to establishing a curriculum because they think it will never be allowed to ever change. Honestly, if this document of curriculum essential skills isn't a living document then that is inherently wrong. Society is ever-changing, and as such, curriculum should be ever-changing, as well.

The next step is to involve a district's board of education. The school board obviously oversees countless financial and staffing decisions, but many times they are never directly involved in many topics involving curriculum and instruction. This is an opportunity lost, and it diminishes the core value of a school system which is to teach kids. I am not suggesting that a school board becomes intimately involved with curriculum decisions as they are not educators. Instead, I am suggesting that this action allows a school board to be made aware in a very formal manner that this is what is being taught. In turn, I think this also estab-lishes the basis for teachers that following the curriculum is an expectation.

As a school opens each fall with the transition of students into a new grade, so should the approval of an updated curriculum of essential skills. Specifically, as each staff collectively prepares prior to the arrival of students, one of the purposes of this work before students arrive should be updating the curriculum's essential skills as necessary. Then a school board should actually have this document be an action item for their approval. In a lot of ways, I can think of no more important docu-ment for the entity tasked with overseeing a school district to approve. Giving the list of curriculum essential skills this scope of importance solidifies its existence and the subsequent expectation that it should also be followed. Without a valid and high-quality curriculum, no real actions can be taken to then improve instruction.

32

QUALITY PD DESCRIPTOR #3 – CREATE A CULTURE OF IMPROVEMENT AND UTILIZATION OF RESEARCH

*T*he next step in the process is ensuring there is the existence of the right type of instructional culture for improvement. At this point, it is important to really stress that these steps are meant to be progressive in nature. In other words, you need to have an objective goal intended to move a district forward and a curriculum that is obviously valid, but most importantly exists.

Once these foundational steps have been taken, then a staff is more ready to accept and understand the notion that decisions need to be based upon research. Every possible problem that a district can have to embrace and work to solve already has research that exists that can help staff members to implement solutions. In addition, we are at the point in our field that quality instruction that aligns to both engagement and student achievement is not a mystery or matter of opinion.

Instruction that is conceptually based in which students are tasked with applying their knowledge correlates to achievement. On the other hand, instruction that aligns with rote memorization in which students remember specific facts that could be obtained through an internet search engine does not. In many ways, establishing this norm should be that simple, and it only becomes more complicated when it is allowed to be.

The best and easiest manner in which to build and ensure there is a culture of improvement is to ensure professional development days with staff are considered the single most important item a district should plan for. In addition, all professional development should predominantly be based on instruction, or a topic directly related to instruction. If this perspective is communicated and driven through action by the leaders of a district this core value will become a part of the learning environment.

However, any successful instructional culture has to include a positive student and staff culture. This realization is not lost upon me. My point is that a positive climate will only take a school so far. For a school to reach its potential, it has to include a culture that connects with instructional improvement.

33

ADMINISTRATORS HAVE TO LEAD PROFESSIONAL DEVELOPMENT

*A*lmost all educational administrators take the same path before becoming a leader for a school or district. The dramatic majority begin their life as a teacher. While the grade level and content may differ significantly, the starting point is almost always the same. They are individuals that enter a career field as a teacher who initially aims at discovering and working towards quality instructional practices for the benefit of students.

As an educator then potentially climbs that field towards an administrative role, they need to always remember what their overarching core of impact was when they began as a teacher. Ideally, it was built upon always working towards improvement as an instructor. While a district administrator will obviously have a wide array of responsibilities, they have to remember how they can have an impact on all of their teachers directly through improving teaching practices.

District administrators have to contribute and lead professional development. They need to model that instruction is a passion of theirs, and even more importantly, that they have the expertise to improve everyone else's. I understand that administrators have a lot of responsibilities, but they need to avoid being totally lost within aspects such as finance, building infrastructure, or human resources. No matter what the set-up or size of a district, each administrator needs to have some type of role for improving instruction.

34

ALL EDUCATORS SHOULD SEE THEMSELVES AS INSTRUCTIONAL COACHES

I understand, acknowledge, and agree with all of the research behind instructional coaches. I have seen the power behind it...if it is done correctly. Educators, like all other individuals, get better when they receive feedback on how to improve when it is done through safe measures outside of evaluations, and that is what should be the intended and core purpose behind coaching someone to improve as an instructor. However, I think the mistake is made in the field of education when instructional coaches are tasked with duties that should be for administrators.

Like any staff, there will naturally be some individuals that perform better than others. The main variable is how administration chooses to address and handle the staff that needs their performance to improve. First, administrators and staff need to have the type of atmosphere that it can be acknowledged that people can and need to improve their craft. There is not a pinnacle point of collective performance that everyone is exemplary. I think everyone knows there is no such thing as this type of reality, but there are also administrators that pretend that they have this type of perfect staff to avoid difficult conversations with teachers that need to get better.

An instructional coach is not an evaluator, but if they are tasked with being responsible for improving a weak teacher that an administrator is not evaluating correctly, then that is exactly what they are being asked to do. This skewed approach to coaching creates a chain reaction that affects professional development and its intended purpose. Individuals will resist improvement and instructional coaches when they are instead utilized as the staff aimed at addressing only the worse performing teachers.

When this approach is used in a school, it perpetuates a negative connotation on all professional development. Instead of having a culture of collective staff inquiry where everyone sees the need to always improve, there will instead be the notion that only the lowest-performing should. Professional development should not be the sole tool to address the low performers that ineffective administrators seek to ignore.

35

DO YOU GIVE ZEROES?

*I*f you are a teacher, or school, that allows the usage of giving students a zero for a missing assignment, this is a practice that is wrong and should be stopped immediately. I am also well aware that taking a position that is so direct on a sensitive topic may be a good way to enrage educators that disagree with me. However, the point I am trying to make is far beyond inciting the endless debate on whether or not teachers should do this.

There is absolutely no research that supports zeroes. None. None whatsoever. For the educators that still support the usage of zeroes, that is your choice and a choice I do not understand. These types of educators have decided that they will be an educator that decides to utilize practices that are outside of what research suggests. I genuinely do not understand this type of reasoning.

This is a very dangerous practice to begin because when does it end? It is easy to look at the recommended conclusions of the research, and then convince oneself that it doesn't apply to them because of whatever reason that seems to fit. It could be because "my kids are different" or "we tried this once already and it didn't work" or anything else that invalidates the recommendation.

I do not have the answer on how an educational leader instantly gets all staff to buy into decisions that could be controversial despite there being a large volume of research that seems to indicate a position. I will probably spend the rest of my career trying to find this solution. However, at this point, I do have two solidified conclusions. One is that having an administrator decide what a practice should be, and then forcing it upon staff is a recipe for disaster with there being no fidelity. Two is that there has to be a culture of, "What does the research indicate?" Acknowledging these two concepts are at least the first step to leading others to the conclusion you wish they would discover on their own.

36

WHAT DOES THE RESEARCH INDICATE?

*L*ike any other person, I have my own personal pet peeves related to the field of education. One occurrence that I find sometimes with school districts that I encounter is that there is little awareness or value put upon research. Practices and policies are driven by past practice perspectives defined by, "This is what we have always done here."

This is a dangerous culture to have because it indirectly establishes that there is no value within a building or district to keep apprised of new and improved ways to benefit students. I am not necessarily stating that staff members need to be all experts that are constantly dissecting current research journals, but there has to be exposure to basic conclusions of practice on various research topics.

For example, round-robin reading is an instructional practice that shows no indication of student engagement or achievement. However, I still see it being utilized from time to time. Upon witnessing this, I always ask myself is this happening because a teacher doesn't know that this practice is a poor one, or do they know, yet not care to change? As I reflect, I really feel the more accurate answer is that some teachers are instead not being exposed to instructional professional development of research-driven instructional practices to consider implementing instead.

37

ARE ALL OF THE TEACHERS AT YOUR SCHOOL PERFECT?

*O*ne of the most obvious and contentious topics at any school district is the topic of evaluations, and in many ways, it will always partially be this way. When one individual is evaluating the performance of another, it will always have a layer of anxiety at a minimum. However, this is a topic where any teachers or administrators that conduct teacher evaluations may have a similar perspective, but in different ways.

Every teacher strives to have the feedback they receive be nothing but exemplary. Who wouldn't want to only hear how great they are? However, I think positive feedback truly only has substance when it is not given to all teachers to avoid difficult conversations. In other words, it would be how a student would feel that initially was proud of an assignment for getting an "A" but then felt a little less significant once they discovered everyone else also got an "A." This would then be compounded more if they knew that other students had not worked as hard as they had.

I see these realities taking place sometimes, and it is a dangerous one. If every teacher is evaluated and deemed as perfect, either because an administrator is scared or incapable of being accurate, it creates a dangerous atmosphere where professional development will not be embraced. In many ways, why would a staff collectively feel that they need to improve and embrace opportunities to do so when every teacher is being evaluated through an approach that everyone is already exemplary?

YOU HAVE TO DO PEER WALKTHROUGHS

I am always a little apprehensive about making recommendations that apply to all educational settings. Every school district is different, and as such, it is difficult to reason that there is ever an approach that should universally be entertained. However, I do feel very strongly that every school has to have a culture in which teachers are constantly being observed, and also observing others.

I can certainly acknowledge all of the variables involved that sometimes makes this type of atmosphere difficult. To exemplify my point, I love asking large groups of teachers how many of them know all sorts of personal traits and attributes about individuals that they work next to. It always amazes and entertains me when they are able to provide these answers sometimes within great detail. However, if this same question is posed, but is asking for teachers to state preferred instructional strategies of the people they work next to, I have usually been met with blank stares and next to no responses. I think this consistent experience clearly demonstrates a point I want to make, and also a sad reality of the field of education.

We somehow seem to have a professional field wherein it is uncommon for educators to observe and learn from each other. This is so much the norm that suggesting a different atmosphere seems quite bizarre, if not scary. If there is one approach to ensure professional development is worthwhile, it has to be a practice that actually is expected to be implemented. Based upon that notion, what is the point of trying to implement a new or improved instructional practice if you have no plan to measure effectiveness? I believe the answer is establishing some type of program in which teachers observe the instruction of other teachers.

Peer walkthroughs should not be evaluative. They should instead be an atmosphere and approach that allows teachers to get honest and safe feedback on their instructional skills. This is true coaching. This is how teachers improve.

QUALITY PD DESCRIPTOR #4 – UTILIZE, EXPECT AND TRAIN ON CONCEPTUAL LEARNING PRACTICES

*O*nce a district has determined that it will function within the approach of achieving goals in an objective manner, have created a formal curriculum, and established a culture of improvement, the last step is to expect teachers to utilize only conceptual learning practices. These steps of building quality professional development need to be built upon each other, and not having any one of them may cause the others to falter. Once a district has gotten to the point of Descriptor #4, this is when buildings can collectively embrace only instructional strategies that are engaging to students and retire the ones that are anything but.

When considering the evolution of instruction, there are two broad spectrums of research. Areas such as physics and chemistry are regarded as the "hard sciences," and work within psychology and education are widely known as the "soft sciences." The hard sciences explore items existing within the natural world while soft sciences are the intangibles and ideas related to the behaviors found in our society. According to Hedges (1987), there is no difference in variability when comparing studies from physics to topics related to the social sciences. Overall, he concluded that research within the "soft sciences" can discover general trends as much as any other research topic and that any finding within a research study in education should be considered the best idea of what is known on such a topic. It is this thinking that helped develop the educational laws and policies that require the use of evidence-based practices.

The realization and acceptance of good instruction being observable and objective is currently a driving force in education. In other words, the idea that teaching is just an art by well-minded adults has been refuted. Charlotte Danielson (1996), an acclaimed educator and researcher in teacher evaluation that so many of us have undoubtedly heard of, commented, "It's not sufficient to say, 'I can't define good teaching, but I know it when I see it.'" Danielson and others in her field have developed frameworks of professional practice, which provide educators with a concrete set of guidelines to follow for research-supported strategies for success.

Theorists such as Dewey, with his ideas on society, democracy, child development, and education, also have had a significant impact on strategies for instruction (Dewey, 1916). With the current information available in modern times on brain development and cognitive functioning, the study of cognitive science is now guiding the discussion of instructional strategies. However, the main point being that there is evidence of what works best to impact students, and what does not.

SO WHAT EXACTLY IS EFFECTIVE
INSTRUCTION?

*I*t is important to note that constructivism is not pedagogy or simply a monolithic and rigid practice meant for all educators to follow for the successful acquisition of knowledge for students. Instead, constructivism is an overall theory of how individuals learn. This theory developed through the observation of learners as modern education has unfolded over the last 150 years; and from this theory, among others, we have reached a point in the field of education theory that there is a generally accepted list of practices on how teachers should teach (Richardson, 1997).

With constructivism being the idea of how people learn, the next step is ensuring there is an understanding that it is also not descriptive towards a manner in which individuals should be taught. Teaching takes place in a variety of settings of which contain a myriad of variables that can be manipulated or are uncontrollable. The idiosyncrasies among individual teachers merit embracing. Nonetheless, as educators strive to create classrooms in which students learn best, the principles of constructivism should be front and center in the instructional planning process (Richardson, 1997).

The outline below indicates the overall characteristics of constructivism and how a teacher utilizing this practice should instruct (Brooks & Brooks, 1993).

- *Encourage and accept student autonomy and initiative.*
- *Use a wide variety of materials, including raw data, primary sources, and interactive materials, and encourage students to use them.*
- *Inquire about students' understandings of concepts before sharing his/her own understanding of those concepts.*
- *Encourage students to engage in dialogue with the teacher and with one another.*
- *Encourage student inquiry by asking thoughtful, open-ended questions and encourage students to ask questions to each other, and seek elaboration of students' initial responses.*
- *Engage students in experiences that show contradictions to initial understandings and then encourage discussion.*
- *Provide time for students to construct relationships and create metaphors.*
- *Assess students' understanding through application and performance of open-structured tasks.*

According to Brooks and Brooks (1993), most teachers view constructivism as the manner in which they have always known students to actually learn. However, the guidelines listed above are not necessarily the approach in which they are allowed to instruct in all settings. Instead, they are prevented from implementing these approaches due to rigid curriculums, issues with administration, and insufficient preparation through poor professional development before leading a classroom.

While the premise of constructivism should be natural and common sense driven according to Brooks and Brooks (1993), many times educators are not given the opportunity to study and embrace the practices. However, they argue that once teachers are exposed, they will many times incorporate becoming a constructivist teacher enthusiastically.

Brooks and Brooks are not the only researchers indicating the inherent drive educators have for embracing these principles. Taking the body of research that has accumulated over the years, educational researcher John Hattie conducted a meta-analysis of more than 800 studies that involved more than 80 million students. His work, *Visible Learning*, is regarded as a checklist for school improvement (Hattie, 2010). Hattie found that the impactful strategies for student success include those grounded in constructivist principles such as inquiry learning, cooperative learning, problem-solving, and, fourth on the list overall, "Piagetian programs." Ultimately, Hattie stated that teachers are the central aspect of a successful learning environment, the instructional strategies they use matter, and there are practices that are substantially more successful to use than others (Hattie, 2010).

41

WHAT ARE THE DIFFERENT TYPES OF INSTRUCTIONAL APPROACHES?

*T*here are a variety of authors and researchers that have defined various types of instruction. While each interpretation has its own merit and worth, I think it is more important to just establish that there are different ones. One such individual that has done this work, who is well known and renowned, would be Robert Marzano.

The work of Marzano has become widely accepted within the field of education as a model for establishing and evaluating the implementation of evidence-based instructional strategies. The goal of his evaluation frameworks and tools is to ensure teachers are having positive effects by using instructional strategies and creating learning environments that are known to be most effective. These build on constructivism and use principles from cognitive science on how the brain processes, encodes, and retrieves information.

Cognitive science is an interrelated branch of scientific study with many similarities to constructivism. Similar to constructivism, cognitive science examines the mind and the processes it incorporates. However, rather than simply focusing on how learning takes place, cognitive science instead examines the functions and tasks involved with overall cognition itself (Bransford, Brown, & Cocking, 2000).

Marzano describes instructional strategies as any factor or action on

the part of the teacher that has some type of effect on student achievement, whether positive or negative. Marzano, Pickering, and Pollock
(2001) developed nine categories of instructional strategies. They include
foundational avenues of classroom practice that a teacher can utilize to
have an impact on student achievement and instructional actions aimed
towards positive results. However, these categories do not indicate strategies specifically meant towards success within particular subject areas,
grade levels, specific students' backgrounds, or differing students' apti-
tudes (Marzano et al., 2001). The list in the next chapter only displays
specific instructor behaviors for each of Marzano et al.'s instructional
categories that are most likely to encourage the development of the
desired student behaviors (Marzano, 2003).

42

MARZANO'S INSTRUCTIONAL STRATEGIES AND THEIR ALIGNMENT TO SPECIFIC BEHAVIORS

*T*here are a variety of researchers and educational leaders that define types of instruction in different ways. While various interpretations no doubt have their own merits, I think it is more important to acknowledge that there are miscellaneous strategies above all else. A lot of teachers rely predominantly on only lecturing to their students. Due to this it then becomes difficult to begin a dialogue on embracing different approaches to impact students if there is not even a basis of understanding that different manners exist. Listed next are the nine instructional strategies as identified by Marzano.

1. ***Identifying Similarities and Differences*** - *Helps learners see patterns and make connections*
2. ***Summarizing and Note Taking*** - *Helps learners analyze content and put it in their own words.*
3. ***Reinforcing Effort and Providing Recognition*** - *Helps learners see the connection between effort and achievement.*
4. ***Homework and Practice*** - *Helps learners learn on their own and apply their new knowledge.*
5. ***Nonlinguistic Representations*** - *Helps learners show content and thinking in ways not limited to verbal representations.*

6. ***Cooperative Learning*** *– Helps learners work together to achieve shared goals.*
7. ***Setting Objectives and Providing Feedback*** *- Helps create personal goals for learners and allows more thoughtful planning by the teacher.*
8. ***Generating and Testing Hypotheses*** *- Guides learners through the process of asking good questions, generating hypotheses and predictions, analyzing data, and communicating results.*
9. ***Questions, Cues, and Advance Organizers*** *- Helps learners connect to what they already know in their existing knowledge prior to presenting new content.*

(Marzano et al., 2001)

What is important to note is that these nine instructional categories have varying levels of effectiveness on the academic progress of students. Put another more simplistic way, is that some of these are more engaging and correlational to student achievement than others. Teachers need to predominantly utilize the ones that are most conceptual for students while being cautious to avoid, or use sparingly, the ones that are driven by simple lecture or direct instruction. An understanding of these various categories is important for both instructors and also individuals leading or planning professional development. If an educator is only aware of some of these instructional categories, it makes the process of instructional improvement only that much more difficult. Individuals cannot improve if they have no idea that there are better, or at least different, ways to impact kids.

Rather than trying to ensure all teachers know every instructional strategy that does not align to the engagement and success of students, it is a much better usage of time to focus on selecting one poor instructional strategy to demonstrate that there are practices that are simply better than others. Take for example the poor instructional approach of just tasking students with memorizing random facts with the main assessment being whether or not a child can then restate the facts at a later point. Earlier in this book, I mentioned the topic of rote memorization being a poor instructional strategy multiple times. I think this topic comes up so frequently because this overarching approach to instruction is still being done in far too many classrooms.

Imagine again you are a student, and now imagine your thoughts towards the teachers that mainly task you to simply memorize facts. It would be an endless endeavor to begin dissecting why this is the approach in so many classrooms, but perhaps a lot of this is based upon that teachers simply do not know any better way, or this was how they were taught. As such, teachers now find themselves copying what they were exposed to when they were students.

No matter what state that a school district is located within, it has learning standards that educators are tasked with ensuring students reach mastery. While each state has its approach to what it identifies as the most important concepts for students to embrace, they do have the universal trait that the standards are not based upon rote memorization. They are built upon areas that students are expected to be able to apply with skills.

Our society has reached a point that no one, including students, needs to focus any large part of their learning on memorizing facts that are absolutely not necessary for skill acquisition. To be extremely specific, classrooms that use large portions of time to challenge students to memorize random historical dates, unnecessary facts, or anything else that is not related to demonstrating or applying knowledge should be avoided. Preparing students for a 21st century world needs to align with teaching them to utilize 21st-century skills.

DO YOU TEACH HOW YOU WERE TAUGHT WHEN YOU WERE A KID, OR HOW YOU WISH YOU WERE TAUGHT?

*G*rowing up everyone naturally had teachers that they liked more than others. There is nothing out of the ordinary about this and it is a part of any educational experience. In other words, some people will naturally connect more with some teachers than others. However, it is interesting to really ask a teacher if they think their current students will describe them as their favorite teacher later in life.

If someone elicits a discussion with any type of educators to ask them to describe the teachers that most impacted them while growing up as a child, they will almost always describe someone that made learning fun. While answers will obviously vary some, the underlying common themes will be a teacher who made them feel welcomed in the classroom. No one ever describes their favorite teacher as the one that drove the classroom by tasking students to memorize facts in a robotic fashion or created a classroom based on compliance of procedures rather than an exploration of interest.

I think a lot can be realized by the fact that a student seems to naturally know what type of classroom that they are drawn to the most, and what type of classroom that they wish they didn't have to attend. If anything, a lot more of the practices and procedures that we implement in public education should be driven by considering this perspective. Do you teach how you were taught when you were a kid, or how you wish you were taught?

44

WOULD STUDENTS ATTEND YOUR CLASS IF THEY DIDN'T HAVE TO?

*A*s I write this book, our world is in the middle of the Covid-19 pandemic. It's been an unprecedented experience that is stressful, overwhelming, and confusing for educators no matter their location and setting. Regardless of where an educator found themselves relative to their readiness to conduct virtual learning, they are in a bizarre new educational world in which students have more autonomy to decide whether or not they choose to engage in their own learning more than ever before.

I have also interacted with countless teachers that found this realization unsettling and even frightening. In many ways, I understand why. When a student had to physically attend in a classroom, they essentially had no choice but to be there. Teachers were then able to build a philosophy of engagement that could have significant layers of compliance.

Teachers then realized that when all learning is done remotely, so much of the decision-making that the educators used to have was no longer there. Instead, students were able to decide when they wanted to learn, the pace they wanted to learn, and the manner in which they wanted to learn. In other words, a lot of the decision-making power had shifted.

Allowing students to learn in a conceptual, self-paced manner while depending on a positive relationship between them and the teacher has always been important. However, these variables are now more important than ever before. A student has a choice on whether or not they want to attend a class with the establishment of virtual learning environments. Some of the best advice I have heard from a variety of sources throughout my career was posing the rhetorical questions to teachers, "If students had a choice, would they choose to attend your class?" We are now living this reality, and if anything, it should exemplify the need to focus upon teaching strategies and professional development that ensures students will do so more than ever before.

Summary

First and foremost, almost all professional development needs to be about instruction. There is nothing more disheartening for an administrator, or more frustrating for a teacher, then wasting time on some type of training that doesn't apply to the intended recipient. Whether a teacher is in charge of preschoolers or advanced calculus, one collective area of focus that applies to all teaching positions is the topic of improving instruction.

At this point, I would not be surprised if anyone is wondering what they should do, or how they should embrace this professional development outline of implementation, based upon where they are at within their own setting. The best way I would answer this would be to remember that being an advocate for a positive climate should be a driving variable no matter where anyone feels that their school or district is at with the four steps of professional development planning.

The outline at the end of this section is meant to be a guide as educators work through a process with a separate and important focus at each step. Step one is creating SMART goals which is when staff realizes that accountability is not a bad thing if done correctly. The professional learning at this point focuses on examining data of student performance to honestly acknowledge areas that need improvement and then creating objective targets to strive for. Step two of creating a curriculum of essential skills needs to be a foundation, but also the point in which teachers realize that concepts that are being taught need to be conceptual and not based on memorization or compliance. These first two steps of this process really can and should be addressed immediately. There is no reason that establishing some type of curriculum, and objective district goals to determine success, could not be done at the start of any given school year.

Step three focuses on creating a culture where all educator's share a core value of instructional improvement, and a culture where teachers see observations as opportunities for feedback, and administrators see themselves as true instructional leaders. The professional learning of this step would be ensuring all staff know what best practice instructional strategies actually are, and working towards all staff having an understanding of terms such as constructivism and the basic concepts brought forth by educational pioneers such as John Dewey.

The last step is continuing to offer professional development for teachers and staff that improves instruction. It could be discussing the concepts of Webb's Depth of Knowledge or providing insight into the Danielson Evaluation Framework. It is just as important at this point for the individuals leading this new learning to be a combination of outside consultants, to provide new perspectives, and in-district leaders, to ensure staff are being empowered. Steps three and four are ongoing and are never truly completed. However, they cannot be addressed until steps one and two are established first.

Professional development plans should be long-term in nature and built upon addressing and improving instruction. This basic purpose never changes, and most importantly, there is never an endpoint. This next graphic outlines the framework to follow. The steps are meant to be followed in order, and lastly, the overall purpose should never change. Improve instruction.

The Professional Development Outline

1 — Step 1 - Have district and building specific SMART goals that are objective, determine success, and address the greatest areas of need.

POSITIVE CLIMATE

Step 2 - Create an established curriculum of essential skills students are expected to learn by grade level and content.

 2

 **3** — Step 3 - Create a culture of accountability by working towards an atmosphere of instructional focus and inquiry based on research.

Step 4 - Use a combination of district personnel, and also outside experts, to train staff on conceptual instructional teaching practices.

 **4**

POSITIVE CLIMATE

 Continually review the process for fidelity and continued improvement with each school year.

By: Dr. Nick Sutton

SECTION 5: BEING AN EDUCATOR IS MORE THAN EDUCATING

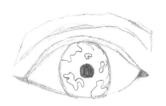

This section is where I am hoping that anyone reading this book sees the connection between the Social Justice Levels of Action and the steps of the Professional Development Outline. An educator needs to honestly self-assess where they are on the Levels of Social Justice Action so they can determine if they are at a place to be able to truly improve. Once that happens, the Professional Development Outline aims to help educators realize that student achievement does not just magically happen. It is driven by improving instruction based upon research while a positive climate is an overarching aim. We all as indi-

viduals have core values that drive us as who we are. While not everyone necessarily realizes that they have their own principles, everyone certainly does. We all make choices every single day, and what we determine as important or not drives these decisions. Educators are, in turn, really no different. We all have our own educational core values, and it is important to really question what they are if it is our goal to ultimately positively impact others.

45

ALL SCHOOLS ARE NOT AWESOME

*E*ducation is the greatest career to be a part of. You get to positively impact lives, be a part of a field that allows networking and continuous growth, and it is also just plain fun. Personally, I think what I find most attractive is with each year that passes, the limitless volume of avenues for improvement increases. There is no such thing as a finish line of performance level, and that never-ending pursuit creates a never-ending challenge.

Every student-teacher enters the field of education ready to change lives and with a volume of confidence that they are going to do things differently and in a way that would have improved the educational experience they had when they were an actual student. Personally, as I finished student teaching, I was fortunate. I had a wonderful mentor teacher during my student teaching experience that supported me, and then when I got that first job, I couldn't have been more excited.

Like everyone else, I had my own professional learning curves when I began teaching, but I lived through these tough experiences and came out fortunate. However, that isn't always the case and is an indirect reason that instructional professional development needs to be the core of a successful school. Some schools that do not have that as a driving value may have different, less than positive, values that are instead built upon acceptance of past practice building norms. They may have staff that are in the "Indifference Level" of Social Justice Levels of Action and have professional development that is anything but organized or instructionally focused.

My first teaching position ended up being a profound experience for a lot of different reasons. I was hired to teach at a middle school that had many admirable qualities. I was thrilled to obtain this position, and even though there ended up being some very tough lessons that I learned, it was an experience that made me improve in ways I never would have anticipated.

The school was unusual in that many of the teachers were tasked with co-teaching with another teacher responsible for the same grade level and content. For example, some of the multiple co-teaching setups included two individuals teaching math to seventh-graders or two individuals teaching language arts to eighth-graders. I can still recall how nervous I was to begin teaching for the first time, so imagining this level of support with having a partner to lesson plan and instruct together sounded so attractive to me.

I truly envisioned scenarios where this individual and I would discuss teaching strategies to impact hard-to-reach students and evaluating new unit plans to engage students in interesting ways. However, I discovered quickly that this was not the expectation or goal of my new co-teaching partner. It was initially explained to me that the basic setup of this teaching partnership would consist of instructing two classes at once in a large classroom. One teacher would lead the full class while the other teacher would assist struggling small groups of students, but be fluid throughout the room to help where it is necessary.

When the first day of school finally arrived, I was so motivated to try to be fantastic. I was driven to want to make an impact in as many ways as possible. It did not take long though to realize that how I envisioned the school year evolving was very different than how my teaching partner did. The first couple of weeks there were indicators that brought me concern, but after a quarter of the school year was complete, I knew that I was teaching with an individual that was at the "Indifference Level" of Social Justice Levels of Action, and maybe due to this, had no interest in improving or even considering doing anything differently.

When my partner taught, I would walk around the classroom monitoring behavior, engaging with students that needed help, and just assisting wherever I saw was necessary. To my dismay though, the slow but deliberate evolution of the setup when I would teach was that my partner would sit at her desk, read a book, and even sometimes make meaningless personal phone calls. She would completely disconnect from being a teacher when I would teach and seeing this did more than make me angry. It made me feel horrendously guilty that this type of school could exist.....and even worse that I was a part of it.

It was a frightening realization that team teaching was actually "take turn teaching." I felt so stuck. As I reflect now at this point in my career, I think I had just not realized that there were educators that were driven by core values that were not based upon impacting kids. I tried sharing my concerns with my teaching partner. I told her that if we are both responsible for almost 60 students at once, then there is nothing beneficial by having one of us sitting at our desk doing nothing when the other teaches. While the discussion was more detailed than my summary here, her final comment to me at the conclusion of our discussion is something I still remember to this day. "Nick, I am just not interested in actually teaching all day. If you want to help out the kids when I am teaching that's fine, but when you teach, I am just going to sit at my desk."

Seeing these words now almost 15 years later still brings about feelings of amazement that students go through educational experiences like this. The building administration knew this was the setup of team teaching, and they did nothing to address it, which led me to feeling more confused than anything else. How can anyone accept being a part of a school like this?

During my brief time at this school, I did my best to impact as many students as possible and also was fortunate to develop some lifelong friendships with a few teachers that were awesome because they had made the decision to be awesome on their own. This school was filled with individuals that were definitely on the "Indifference Level" though and this perpetuated into anything but professional development that positively impacted instruction. The school improvement days at one point literally had a veteran teacher sitting at a table knitting while mildly interested administrators were presenting state testing data to point out areas of deficiency, but offering zero input on how to actually improve.

I felt like the culture of this school was one of anything besides improving instructionally for the benefit of students. This was a school that would have to examine its collective core values before and during the implementation of planning quality professional development. In so many ways, it doesn't matter what plans for improvement are created unless and until issues like the one above are addressed. This school serves as an example of why the professional development outline indicates climate as the outside variable that must always have a focus.

46

SOME SCHOOLS HAVE PROFESSIONAL DEVELOPMENT ALL WRONG

*W*hen discussing professional development, there are also school districts that certainly appear at the surface level to be doing everything right. They offer professional development that is based upon improving instruction and have an inherent focus upon examining data to improve student performance. I initially thought the district of one of my beginning administrative positions as a principal had a lot figured out, but what I was soon to discover was that I was wrong.

This setting first made me learn a powerful lesson that individuals cannot improve if their core values are no more than just trying to align new staff members to the "Indifference Level" of addressing social injustices. Unfortunately, though, it is an entirely different level when an educator is truly racist, and this school had some educators that certainly were. As I reflect now so many years later, I still wonder if individuals outside of education completely realize that there are educators that are legitimately and honestly racist, yet get to work with kids.

One of the first things I did as the new leader of the building was to examine the data myself. My initial concern was the huge volume of students that were failing and also being expelled. Most concerning though was the glaringly apparent common variable that almost every one of these students was African American. There were some teachers that were wonderful, some that tried hard, but there were some that were undeniably and unequivocally indifferent that almost every student that failed or constantly was in trouble in their class was African-American.

Trying to address this only broadened my fears when I would hear comments, "We simply have high expectations," and even worse, "We never wanted these kids in our school anyways." I can still recall sitting absolutely dazed in my office wondering how I am supposed to improve instruction when there was such a glaringly ugly building norm that all kids not only won't succeed but cannot succeed. While I ultimately am very proud of being able to address some of the disturbing practices some of the staff had, it made me realize the significance climate has on not being able to improve instruction. I saw firsthand that while a climate ideally will be positive, it can also be very much toxic.

This setting also made me realize the significance of step four of my professional development outline. There was no expectation of what curriculum to teach, no utilization of research to drive decisions, and professional development suggesting any type of change was resisted at all costs. In other words, there was anything but an instructional climate or any type of collective positive atmosphere for students. It is so important that professional learning is led by a combination of both in-house staff members and also outside of the district collaborators. This district was the epitome example of why this point is paramount to ensure professional learning is both worthwhile and meaningful.

One staff member, for reasons that I will never understand, had decided all professional development had to be led by her. No matter the topic, direction, or intended goal the training had to be led by her, or she would sabotage, belittle, and ensure the professional development was not successful. As near as I could tell, her driving principle seemed to be a combination of toxic ambition and a need to reassure herself of her own personal worth.

Professional development should not be a "singular" or a "title." Instead, it should be a "collective" and a "movement." All staff members need to positively impact the improvement of their peers, and new ideas have to be brought in from outside of a district to ensure new perspectives are constantly being revealed. When a district simply allows one person, or a very small group, to control all professional improvement, it provides a significant opportunity for an issue. I saw firsthand how having a toxic individual that controls and impacts all professional development of a district negatively affects every other aspect of a school. It allowed racist teachers to go unaddressed, and instructional improvement to never get the focus that it should have. In other words, it can appear at face value to be worthwhile to train someone on how to replace a flat tire on a car, but it is not appropriate to have that be the entire focus when the engine is blown up.

47

SOME SCHOOLS GET IT RIGHT

ortunately, the vast majority of schools are ones with values-driven towards helping students and the vast majority of educators are wonderful people that do incredible things every day to positively impact lives. While the journey that has been my career has had a couple of experiences that had some individuals and values that were incredibly disappointing, these places still had more good than bad in their own distinctive ways. In addition, when considering all of the places I have worked at or collaborated with, the majority have been predominantly wonderful. It's amazing reflecting upon all of the fantastic educators that I have encountered, and at this point, I can really see some of the common variables that these people shared.

One school that I was privileged enough to lead as a principal was such a positive place that I use the term privileged very purposefully. It was at this place that I saw the Levels of Action for Social Justice in action. I constantly witnessed individuals existing within the "Action Level" of purpose. This building had a culture in which supporting families at all costs was a collective expectation, and ensuring all students were successful was an unshakable principle. One of my previous experiences as a principal discussed earlier had a group of educators where the contrasting view was the norm. Being able to witness the polar opposite experience made me realize the insignificance of only words and the power of action.

These experiences also made me see that for true instructional improvement to take place through professional development, a staff has to collectively be at a level of truly wanting to positively impact all students. And once that point has been reached, that is when the Professional Development Outline can have a huge impact. Now even though I could provide a variety of examples of professional learning that took place at this school, I instead find myself driven to point out its greatest quality. A positive climate.

This school is the reason that the Professional Development Outline has a never-ending focus on climate as an included component. The teachers met daily as grade-level teams to discuss ways to reach students, had an interest in discussing curriculum for its continued improvement, and there was a collective expectation that all professional development would be built to improve instructional practices.

However, it is still the positive climate that I witnessed firsthand here that makes me realize this is what led to this place's success. There was never a time that a student wasn't greeted while passing in the hallway, a month that did not have some type of fun pep assembly or a day that a staff member didn't do something that reminded me of why I felt lucky to be a part of this team. This school got it right in so many ways. While it probably is possible that professional development can have at least some type of impact regardless of climate, it will never have the impact that it could unless it was as outstanding as this school was.

48

IS AN EDUCATORS' VOLUME OF WORK SYNONYMOUS WITH A LACK OF HAPPINESS?

I have been to a lot of conferences and have heard a lot of different individuals discuss leadership. One topic that always seems to come up as a conversational piece is a presumption that working a high volume of hours is somehow always a bad thing. Essentially, the notion seems to be that if an educator works too much, this is negative.

I am in no way naive that there is such a thing as not taking enough time for one's own personal life with the demands of educational leadership. I have been a victim of mixing up and making the mistake of engaging in an unhealthy ratio of work and personal life balance. However, the question I have begun to enjoy posing to others is why is a heavy workload always a bad thing?

I like what I do. I think the work is important. I find value in what I do. However, most importantly I am happiest when the culture I am working in is built upon doing what is best for students, and that type of culture makes working a high number of hours enjoyable and a passion.

One of the main variables I like when potentially hiring someone is to discover what their core values are. I want to know what is important to them and what drives them. This includes discovering these traits both personally and professionally. Related to this concept is my belief that school climate is dependent in a lot of ways on whether or not a large group of people all have the same core values in the setting they find themselves in. This is where collective goals to improve through best practice instructional strategies is key.

If an educator can put themselves in a school building that has core values that matches their own, they will be happy. I don't think there is necessarily a "thing" as being too involved with my work. Educators should ideally find satisfaction in what they do, and this will then bring happiness into their life.

Whether I like it or not, the balance between my personal and professional life is definitely intermingled and the line between the two is ambiguous. However, I have realized I like it this way and that this is a good thing because my professional life brings me personal value.

If an individual is in a setting and doing work that matches their core values, I am hesitant when someone else tells them that there is such a thing as too much of that experience. Life is about finding purpose, and finding that purpose in a professional setting is something I found for myself. I truly believe it is only when a school has too many staff members that do not see the value of constantly improving for the benefit of students, that this will heavily burden the other staff members that have the opposite perspective. It is these types of environments that I believe create realities where not just too much work time, but any amount of work time can actually be detrimental.

49

GOOD TEST SCORES OR GOOD INSTRUCTION?

I think many individuals look at test scores to determine and "judge" whether or not a school is doing a good job. This practice has been pretty well established as both a norm and also acceptable within our own society as a whole. I feel as though my opinion is pretty well supported by the actions of legislators. No matter the state, it seems that they are always basing new ideas on using these types of assessments as the means to determine if new funding or mandates for schools were worthwhile.

Many educators have issues with this type of correlation between testing and school performance. This reservation is with good reason since this type of assessment of a school is very subjective. However, I have also reached the conclusion that simply stating this isn't a fair or good practice is also missing the larger point. If a school does happen to be doing well on some type of state assessment, this is something a school will then be proud to acknowledge and advertise. However, why are schools proud of test scores, but not necessarily proud of their instructional strategies through quality professional development?

I have never personally seen a school advertise on their website that they only utilize best practice instructional strategies, but I have certainly seen schools advertise their arbitrary standardized test scores. I am starting to believe this lack of correct emphasis is not only part of the problem, but also reflective of a core value that needs to shift within all educators as a whole.

I have seen many educators make comments in a variety of settings that they wish there was not the emphasis and inaccurate conclusion of how well a school is doing with standardized test scores. However, few have been able to discover the manner in which to make this shift occur. Perhaps, this could happen if all educators saw the value of only utilizing best practices, and then proudly claiming that they only do so.

Individuals that work within education understand the fallacy of defining a school based upon a test, but an individual outside of education simply may not. Since we as public educators are not advertising good instruction as being paramount, maybe this is part of the problem of why quality professional development does not get the emphasis that it should.

50

WHAT INSTRUCTIONAL STRATEGIES DO TEACHERS USE?

*W*hen I was fully in the midst of finishing my dissertation and working towards trying to discover the results that I thought I would find, a part of the process was collecting data of what instructional strategies do teachers actually utilize. Now, are these results applicable without question to every classroom setting out there? Absolutely not. However, they do present a starting point for dialogue of what teachers typically do, and how this can be taken into consideration when planning professional development.

Specifically, the results showed that almost all teachers used all nine categories of instruction at least once a month as identified by Marzano, previously mentioned in this book. This list of the nine categories of instruction are displayed again as follows.

MARZANO'S INSTRUCTIONAL STRATEGIES AND THEIR ALIGNMENT TO SPECIFIC BEHAVIORS

1. *Identifying Similarities and Differences - Helps learners see patterns and make connections*

2. **Summarizing and Note Taking** - *Helps learners analyze content and put it in their own words.*

3. **Reinforcing Effort and Providing Recognition** - *Helps learners see the connection between effort and achievement.*

4. **Homework and Practice** - *Helps learners learn on their own and apply their new knowledge.*

5. **Nonlinguistic Representations** - *Helps learners show content and thinking in ways not limited to verbal representations.*

6. **Cooperative Learning** – *Helps learners work together to achieve shared goals.*

7. **Setting Objectives and Providing Feedback** - *Helps create personal goals for learners and allows more thoughtful planning by the teacher.*

8. **Generating and Testing Hypotheses** - *Guides learners though the process of asking good questions, generating hypotheses and predictions, analyzing data, and communicating results.*

9. **Questions, Cues, and Advance Organizers** - *Helps learners connect to what they already know in their existing knowledge prior to presenting new content.*

(Marzano et al., 2001)

My personal research indicated that the most frequently used were strategies that allowed for elaboration and using learned skills with feedback from the teacher. These include *questions, cues, and advance organizers* and *reinforcing effort, and providing recognition*. According to Marzano, these help learners connect what they already know to the newly learned content and help learners see the connection between effort and achievement. The categories used the least were *homework and practice* and *generating and testing hypotheses*. Marzano describes homework as having learners apply and practice their knowledge and skills on their own. Generating hypotheses involves having learners ask good questions, make predictions, analyze data, and communicate results.

However, the teachers that did indicate that they used *homework and practice* frequently demonstrated interesting findings to consider. Specifically, of the nine categories of instruction as defined by Marzano, all significantly correlated with each other except for *homework and practice*. In other words, teachers that indicated heavy usage of any of the other eight instructional strategies also indicated relatively heavy usage of all of the others, as well, except for *homework and practice*.

Teachers that indicated a heavy usage of *homework and practice* as an instructional strategy only then indicated heavy usage to one other instructional strategy. This was *summarizing and note-taking*. Essentially, my data showed that teachers that give lots of homework and build classrooms based upon it also will apparently use lots of time having students take notes. In contrast, teachers that use cooperative learning as a staple of their learning approach seemed to then use many of the other instructional approaches, except for a focus on homework.

These results confirmed a lot of my preconceived notions that I have gathered during my own educational career. Essentially, a teacher that utilizes hands-on and conceptual learning strategies does not utilize homework and practice nearly as much. However, a teacher that profoundly utilizes homework and practice does not seem to use many other instructional strategies. I sometimes truly do think that teachers that have classrooms in which all they primarily do is lecture, have students take notes, and then assign homework is because they know no other way. The data of my research also seems to support this. I believe this realization may not surprise many, but to me, it solidified the need for professional development to be based upon the outline described in this book. Some teachers are simply not utilizing instructional strategies that are engaging and aligned with student achievement. Why this is not happening may not be critical to understand or discover. Instead, the focus just needs to be based on changing these types of classrooms for the benefit of students.

51

WHAT DID MY RESEARCH INDICATE ABOUT BUILDING A POSITIVE CLIMATE?

*A*s mentioned early in this book, I was initially convinced that some instructional strategies would correlate to both student achievement and also a positive climate. It was my goal to identify teaching strategies, that in my mind, would be impossible not to justify using in a school. However, I did realize one conclusion that is necessary to consider when building professional development plans.

Administrative support correlates to a positive climate. This claim is certainly not anything new, or something that would be surprising to many. What did surprise me personally was that having a school in which teachers indicated that they felt supported by their administration was the only real variable that impacted climate. No instructional strategies showed any indication that they ever directly affected a school's atmosphere whatsoever.

The underpinning hypothesis of my research was that certain instructional practices would be related to a positive school climate. The assumption was that instructional strategies which were hands-on and collaborative in nature would exist more predominantly in school settings that teachers reported as having positive attitudes and cultures. This was based on my initial idea that activities in a classroom that required collaboration and engaging in personal interactions would align to a trend of collaboration and engagement school-wide. In many ways, this initial position was somewhat simplistic as the relationship among these factors likely involves more complex interrelationships.

The results of my work and experiences indicated that if teachers felt supported by their administrative team then there will be a positive atmosphere. As school administrators select various approaches or initiatives to focus upon, the data from my research would support recommending they utilize supportive actions with a teaching staff if the overall goal is building and sustaining a positive climate. However, one clear point that needs to be made is that my research study aimed to discover if the relationship between the two existed, and are not to imply that they are cause and effect in nature.

I think this is so important to realize because if the overarching greatest area of need for a school or district is improving the culture, quality professional development based upon instruction will likely not address it. I began having the wishful thinking mindset that trying to improve one area would magically have a relational effect on other areas of a school, as well, but that was not my findings.

Teachers and administrators need to be hesitant to conclude that any instructional selection will lead to a difference in school climate. Instead, school climate will only be impacted through interventions directly aligned to making such changes. If a school staff is aiming to improve student achievement, then professional development needs to align to improving instruction. If a school staff is aiming to improve school culture, then professional development needs to align to improving culture, and administrative support appears to be one of the best approaches.

52

BE HESITANT TO PRESUME ANY CORRELATIONAL RELATIONSHIPS WHEN ATTEMPTING TO MAKE CHANGE

So often schools and districts implement programs aimed at becoming the "silver bullet" that will fix all of their issues. The reasoning seems to be that if they focus on fixing one problem, then perhaps it will magically fix other issues, as well. I obviously fell into this trap myself when working on my own dissertation study. I was convinced that there would be specific instructional strategies that would also be "silver bullets." I thought there would be strategies that engaged classrooms, made students learn, and also would create a climate where everyone was happy. At the time, I thought I was on to a fascinating concept, but I see now that I was perhaps a bit naive. For example, if I implemented an after-school tutoring program for students, would it make any sense if I thought this would help address if there was also an issue of some teachers still using poor instructional strategies? The answer is of course not, but still, I see these types of mistakes take place in schools all the time.

We simply have to be apprehensive about the assumptions of any correlational relationships. As educators make decisions to implement plans to impact student achievement, climate, or various other endeavors, it is worthwhile to consider the results of my study and point of view.

Interventions that are selected to impact a specific goal should not be accompanied by the assumption that it will necessarily have broad impacts on other areas, as well.

53

ENTERTAIN IDEAS. DON'T DISMISS THEM

We work in a field in which every piece of research can be argued or subjectively debated. So many times I hear instances in which an educator is told what the research indicates, and then presented with the data on why the change should occur. However, instead of embracing the notion, they instead portray arbitrary reasons why their classrooms, school, or district is "different" and the research simply does not apply to them. This notion is a large part of the section of this book that discusses why some educators resist improvement through professional development.

I am challenging everyone reading this book to do the latter. I am not implying that my point of view and interpretation of the research is perfection and an answer to solve all educational issues. I am instead challenging everyone to simply embrace and consider what I am putting out there has worked for me, and perhaps it could work for you. In other words, perhaps the "silver bullet" in education to universally improve student achievement is to create the collective climate that new ideas are not seen as opportunities to refute, but instead, they are seen as opportunities to consider. Even further, maybe new ideas should be seen as opportunities that could provide the same level of success for others that they did for the author.

. . .

Summary

Educators in this field are obligated to ensure academic growth and achievement for all students under their responsibility. Each state within the United States has some type of learning standards that serves as a guideline of expectations for teachers to strive for. In addition to an expectation of learning as outlined at a state level, this expectation is shared at the federal level, as well.

The field of education has a lot at stake when considering the purpose of improving practice. The very premise of education is achievement and improvement about something much larger than just a product. It is about the achievement and improvement of children's lives. Professional development is unbelievably important, so much so that an administrator working with a teaching staff to modify their instructional practices in any way should be driven by the notion that this is the most direct way to also positively affect the achievement of students.

This book is a blueprint of an idea. It is an idea that provides a direction for people to follow, and ideas that are meant to solve problems should be accompanied with an open mind. The field of education is not an easy one. When working with children and their futures, it is a sensitive topic for all of the reasons that people can imagine. However, the more that all educators can embrace just how challenging our jobs are, the more that we can perhaps build a reality in which we help each other.

I love the education field so much. As I realize at this point in my life that I am about halfway done with my career, I begin to contemplate how I think I could hopefully impact it more broadly. Beginning educators work towards determining their core values, and then as the years go by, the next transition is trying to reach conclusions of practice for the remainder of their career. The difference though between this professional field and others is that we are working within the precious area of people's lives. As I continue to work on finding my best place of personal and professional happiness, I think I have learned the following. Being responsible for children's futures can make you anxious. Working in the field that is your passion can drive you crazy. However, discovering the happy medium is where you blissfully survive.

REFERENCES

Adelman, J. (2018, January 10). Why the idea that the world is in terminal decline is so dangerous – Jeremy Adelman | Aeon Ideas. Retrieved January 10, 2018, from https://aeon.co/ideas/why-the-idea-that-the-world-is-in-terminal-decline-is-so-dangerous

Archer, D. (2017, February 18). Declinism: Why You Think America is in Crisis. Retrieved January 31, 2018, from https://www.psychologytoday.com/blog/reading-between-the-headlines/201702/declinism-why-you-think-america-is-in-crisis

Brooks. J.G. & Brooks, M.G. (1993) *In search of understanding: The case for constructivist classrooms*. Alexandria, VA: American Society for Curriculum Development.

Bransford, J. D., Brown, A. L., & Cocking, R. R. (2000). *How people learn: Brain, mind, experience, and school*. Washington DC: National Academy Press.

Cremin, L. A. (1961). *Transformation of the school*. Knopf.

Danielson, C. (1996). *Enhancing professional practice: A framework for teaching*. Alexandria, VA: Association for Supervision and Curriculum Development.

Darling-Hammond, L., & Rothman, R. (2015). *Teaching in the flat world: Learning from high-performing systems*. New York, NY: Teachers College Press.

Dewey, J. (1916). *Democracy and education*. New York, NY: Macmillan.

Etchells, P. (2015, January 16). Declinism: Is the world actually getting worse? *The Guardian*. Retrieved February 07, 2018, from https://www.theguardian.com/ science/head-quarters/2015/jan/16/declinism-is-the-world-actually-getting-worse

Glasersfeld, E. V. (n.d.). Learning and adaptation in the theory of constructivism. *Critical Readings on Piaget, 20-27.*

Hattie, J. (2010). *Visible learning: A synthesis of over 800 meta-analyses relating to achievement*. London: Routledge.

Hedges, L. V. (1987). How hard is hard science, how soft is soft science? The empirical cumulativeness of research. *American Psychologist, 42* (5), 443-455.

Hickman, L. A., Reich, K., & Neubert, S. (2013). *John Dewey between pragmatism and constructivism*. New York, NY: Fordham University Press.

Kliebard, H. M. (2004). *The struggle for the American curriculum, 1893-1958* (3rd ed.). New York, NY: RoutledgeFalmer.

Kozulin, A. (2007). *Vygotsky's educational theory in cultural context.* UK: Cambridge University Press.

Marzano, R. J., Pickering, D. J., & Pollock, J. E. (2001). *Classroom instruction that works: Evidence-based strategies for increasing student achievement.* Boston, MA: Pearson Education.

Marzano, R. J. (2003). *What works in schools: Translating research into action.* Alexandria, VA: Association for Supervision and Curriculum Development.

Nash, R. J. (1996). *"Real world" ethics: Frameworks for educators and human service professionals.* New York, NY: Teachers College Press.

Palmer, P. J. (2011). *Healing the heart of democracy: the courage to create a politics worthy of the human spirit.* San Francisco, CA: Jossey-Bass.

Piaget, J. (1978). *Psychology and epistemology: Towards a theory of knowledge.* Markham, Ont.: Penguin Books.

Piaget, J., & Inhelder, B. (1969). *The psychology of the child.* New York, NY: Basic Books.

Piaget, J., Smith, L., & Brown, T. (2011). *Sociological studies.* London, England: Routledge.

Richardson, V. (1997). *Constructivist teacher education: Building new understandings.* London, England: Falmer Press.

Thomas, M. H. (1962). *John Dewey: A centennial bibliography.* Chicago, IL: University of Chicago Press.

Vygotsky, L., Davidov, V., & Silverman, R. (1997). *Educational psychology.* Boca Raton, FL: St. Lucie Press.

Vygotsky, L. S., Cole, M., Stein, S., & Sekula, A. (1978). *Mind in society: The development of higher psychological processes.* Cambridge, MA: Harvard University Press.

ABOUT THE AUTHOR

Dr. Nick Sutton resides in the Chicago, Illinois area. His passions include instruction, school improvement, and school climate. He can be found on Twitter @DrNickSutton.

EduMatch

PUBLISHING

Made in the USA
Monee, IL
06 May 2022

96015057R00098